‖‖‖ ‖ ‖‖‖‖‖‖‖ ‖ ‖‖ ‖ ‖‖‖‖‖‖‖‖‖‖‖ ‖‖
W9-BCG-075

PN   Wolseley, Roland Edgar.
4877   The changing magazine;
.W56   trends in readership and
        management.

PN   Wolseley, Roland Edgar.
4877   The changing magazine;
.W56   trends in readership and
        management.

89022028

THE DAVID GLENN HUNT
MEMORIAL LIBRARY
Galveston College
Galveston, Texas

DAVID GLENN HUNT
MEMORIAL LIBRARY
GALVESTON COLLEGE

Studies in Media Management

A. William Bluem, General Editor

The Changing Magazine

TRENDS IN READERSHIP AND MANAGEMENT

Studies in Media Management

BROADCAST MANAGEMENT
Radio-Television
by
Ward L. Quaal and Leo A. Martin

CLASSROOM TELEVISION
New Frontiers in ITV
by
George N. Gordon

CASE STUDIES IN BROADCAST MANAGEMENT
by
Howard W. Coleman

THE MOVIE BUSINESS
American Film Industry Practice
Edited by
A. William Bluem and Jason E. Squire

THE CHANGING MAGAZINE
Trends in Readership and Management
by
Roland E. Wolseley

The Changing Magazine

Trends in Readership and Management

by

ROLAND E. WOLSELEY

Communication Arts Books

Hastings House, Publishers · New York

DAVID GLENN HUNT
MEMORIAL LIBRARY
GALVESTON COLLEGE

To the Students in the
Magazine Seminar
Where so Many of the
Ideas in This Book
Were Discussed

Copyright © 1973 by Roland E. Wolseley

All rights reserved. No part of this publication may be reproduced,
stored in a retrieval system, or transmitted, in any form or by
any means, electronic, mechanical, photocopying, recording or otherwise,
without the prior permission of the publishers.

Library of Congress Cataloging in Publication Data

Wolseley, Roland Edgar. Date. The changing magazine.

  (Studies in media management) (Communication arts books)
  Bibliography: p.
  1. American periodicals.   I. Title.
PN4877.W56   051   73-67
ISBN 0-8038-1179-9

Published simultaneously in Canada by
Saunders of Toronto, Ltd., Don Mills, Ontario

Printed in the United States of America

Contents

Acknowledgments

To Dr. A. William Bluem, editor of this series, my thanks for his encouraging me to develop this book.

To the following persons or organizations my thanks for permission to use certain materials:

Professor Edmund C. Arnold, designer of many leading newspapers and magazines and chairman of the Graphic Arts Department, the School of Public Communications of Syracuse University, who prepared many of the cartoons especially for this book.

Change Magazine, New Rochelle, New York.

Industrial Marketing Magazine, Chicago, Illinois

The New Yorker, New York.

The Saturday Evening Post, Indianapolis, Indiana.

Wil-Jo Associates, Inc., and Bill Mauldin, Chicago, Illinois.

R.E.W.

Introduction

TEACHERS OF PUBLIC communications have long been aware of the necessity to maintain proper curricular balance between professional education and traditional liberal arts studies. The recent rise of enrollments in departments and schools of communication, however, has been accompanied by an ever greater demand for more professionalization, bringing into focus once more the question of what constitutes a sound undergraduate education. At some universities technical proficiency outweighs all other considerations. "How-to" and "hands-on" courses proliferate, and the matter of "what should be said to India" is left to be thought about only after each academic division has made certain that the student has skills enough to land his first job. Teachers who pay loudest tribute to the value of broad education are often busily engaged in piling on more required skills courses —usually with the eager encouragment of professional societies.

Young people can hardly be faulted for having such exclusive interest in mastering the skills and techniques which may lead to immediate (and glamorous) reward in the contemporary media. Nor can administrators be blamed for failing to resist the realities of undergraduate enrollment figures in courses which promise such mastery—particularly when media practitioners invade the campus in droves, demanding that things be taught as they have found them to be in "the real world." As a result of this combination of pressures, professionalism—with all of its limitations in philosophic outlook, its jargon, and its intellectual inbreeding—has come to dominate the educational experience of future communicators in our society.

In this situation the possibilities for creating human obsolescence are ignored—despite the growth in number and variety of media and media-systems, and regardless of the variety of new and independent forms and styles which have been introduced into the communicative act and process. One might assess the impact of changes in dissemination technology upon academic specialization by asking where writers of radio drama and creators of photojournalistic essays might turn for employment now that the major media for which such skills were required—national network radio and the great photojournalism magazines—have fallen into obscurity.

At what point, then, can the university escape this vicious circle which has been drawn by technicians of professionalization (from media as well as communications faculties) and the realities of undergraduate student interest? Clearly, the battle must be joined within those departmental and college faculties where standards have been allowed to slide and where long-range interests of the student have been sacrificed. Now, more than ever before, communications educators must take charge again. Teachers, collectively and individually, must assume a dual obligation: first to education of the whole person, and—of equal significance—to professional training of a breadth and range which assures a reasonable flexibility and mobility to the young professional entering the field. We are, after all, speaking of nothing less than the education of those who will command the attention of an entire civilization for the remainder of this incredible century.

The author of this volume holds such a dual commitment. A staunch defender of traditional liberal arts studies as basic to the education of complete human beings, Roland Wolseley has also earned an honored reputation as a teacher of breadth and vision in the field of journalism. His conviction in the rightness of both kinds of education has led him to prepare a volume which assures perpetuation of high standards in professional preparation. By reviewing the awesome changes which have come over the magazine as an industry and socio-cultural force in American life, Professor Wolseley has given to students some valuable insights into how they may best prepare themselves for meaningful and useful careers in the field.

A. WILLIAM BLUEM
Professor of Media Studies
Syracuse University

Preface

READERS OF MAGAZINES in the United States form a large group. Eighty-nine per cent of all men and women 18 years of age or older read such publications, according to a 1972 report of W.R.Simmons, the media research firm. About 116 million adults each read an average of eight different issues a month or, as the Magazine Publishers Association puts it, "nearly everyone reads magazines."

Since periodicals are such an important institution in the life of our nation, someone ought to take stock of them. Are they doing the job they should? What are their weaknesses and strengths, virtues and faults? How do readers react to them? Are our periodicals fighting for the basic freedoms and other vital causes? How and why are magazines changing? What is the direction of these changes? Will they survive in the communications race? These are some of the questions faced in the pages ahead.

So far as I have been able to discover, this book is the first to be devoted wholly to a critical examination of the magazines of America. My intention has been to go beyond the descriptive volumes about magazines which I and others have produced. The objective has been to present certain facts, ideas and opinions that have come out in discussions with people in the industry, colleagues, students and general readers. Therefore, no how-to-do-it material and only a few technical details about the magazine industry appear here.

My hope is that readers of this book will enjoy their magazines more, expect more from them, make known their reactions to publishers and bring constructive criticism to bear upon them.

R.E.W.

The Changing Magazine

TRENDS IN READERSHIP AND MANAGEMENT

Magazines have to keep changing. We should not only be reflecting the social changes of the country, but also anticipating tastes and needs of readers.

—OSBORN ELLIOTT
Editor and Chairman of the Board,
Newsweek 1972

1

The Forces for Change

A SUBJECT SURE to bring argument whenever thoughtful journalists or scholars of communications assemble is whether publications mirror public opinion or help to form it. The few studies of magazine influence and content prove nothing conclusive, however, and the discussion generally is grounded when the point is reached that the press in an industrialized country, being primarily a commercial venture, can do no more than its financial supporters will permit.

The political and social colorations of the supporters of magazines—advertisers, investors, owners and consumers—what some people call The Establishment—determine decisions about policy and content. It would be hard to deny that all communications media, not magazines alone, that have defied this Establishment are exceptions. Magazine history is filled with instances of failure of well-meaning crusaders who moved against the grain of managerial policy. Whether it was conservative or liberal reaction made no difference. The resources of the few successful rebels generally are private: university, church, labor union or some other organization subsidy.

Therefore when American magazines are changing, as in the seventh decade of this century, it is likely to be in response to a changing public and to decisions by entrepreneurs to face certain realities for the sake of survival. The shocking losses of famous magazines in recent years, the business decline of many others dependent upon commercial success or upon donors from the general public and the effective challenge for revenue from television, have forced some editors and publishers to consider a new course and even a new format for their periodicals. But most important is their alteration of the editorial formulas—as general interest and women's magazines have done in recognizing, for example, the existence of the ethnic minorities, the women's liberation movement and the youth counter-culture.

THE READER HOLDS THE KEY

Readers—the consumers—are the most vital force for changes, of the many that exist. Without them magazines have neither life nor purpose. Every type of periodical is read by someone, even one intended for tiny children or for the sightless. Some magazines consist of nothing but advertising messages or coupons for cut-rates on groceries, yet they are read. Without readers, and the right number of them, there is no sense in trying to sell advertising space, in soliciting subscriptions or requesting subsidy donations. Writers, editors and illustrators are then jobless so far as magazine employment is concerned. Even those racketeers who dig up scandal about public figures and threaten to print it in their shabby magazines unless the victim pays them off, could not make such threats if there were no readers to depend upon.

If the reader is the key to magazine survival it consequently behooves publishers to pay heed to his desires. During most of American magazine history the readers' demands have been comparatively easy to meet. Entertainment was primarily what was sought. Conventional short stories and novels, jokes, descriptive articles, humorous cartoons, travel tales—sheer escapism—sufficed for most readers, and to a great extent still do. Serious, controversial articles and experimental or off-beat fiction were left to the magazines of certain minorities, such as those supported by church, literary, political and social groups. The large mass "books," as the publishers like to call magazines and which the general public usually has considered all of magazinedom, ignored the dynamite of social issues. Wars were supported blindly, racial atrocities like lynchings ignored, corruption in government taken for granted and barely exposed (if exposed at all) and city slums blamed on the jobless who would not work. No one questioned the polluting of air and water by industry or the marring of the countryside by mining companies and billboard advertisers. No one, that is, except a handful of periodicals published by what their critics liked to call "do-gooders" and "world-savers."

Nor did such questionings command national attention until the muck-raking period of the early years of this century. That era stands out precisely because popular magazines like *McClure's* and *Collier's* were exceptional in their candor and aggressiveness in exposing what they considered the evils of the day. They succeeded, but only temporarily, because that was the mood of the time, the social wave. They helped create that wave, to be sure, but it was the political and religious leaders who were mainly responsible—such critics of the social order as Eugene V. Debs and Henry George. When the social critics were overwhelmed by the hysteria of World War I, domestic reforms were submerged and civil rights were threatened (even denied) to certain publications and individuals, including magazines.

From then on periodicals were affected by new domestic developments as well as new wars: there were economic depressions or recessions, the burgeoning of sports and the amusement world, the spread of escapism on radio and then television. The public's access to more leisure, mass-produced automobiles and the spread of aircraft travel also helped to change magazines. A few periodicals continued to challenge an economic order that produced instability and abused man's inventiveness, but they were low-circulation magazines, including the *Survey, The Nation, The World Tomorrow* and a few on the extreme political left or spokesmen for such traditional doubters as the Quakers.

Television's effects began to be felt by the magazine industry—as the one widely acknowledged force for change in magazines. It was generally thought that television's appeal deprived magazines of their readers and that their troubles stemmed from diminished circulations. Reading did drop, but only during the first few months after installation of a new TV receiving set, when watching the screen was an absorbing and wondrous novelty. Actually, circulations increased over the long run during television's continuing rise.

But the magazines' advertising revenues did decline because of the new popular medium, with the result that they have been hurt ever since (although some recovery has been made). For magazines could not provide a mass audience comparable in size to television's. Only the *Reader's Digest* at any time has come close to the boxcar figures that TV can boast. It took years before advertisers were convinced that magazines might be weaker quantitatively but could prove considerable strength qualitatively.

A disadvantage that hurt the large magazines in particular was the fact that broadcasting companies had a comparatively low cost distribution for their advertising messages. The size of broadcasting's audience could be mammoth without materially boosting the operating cost. But no magazine could double its circulation unless it was prepared to pay large sums for the greater number of copies printed, and distributed, through the mails and newsstands. (See App. 2.)

READERS' REBELLIONS

To the flower children, the rebel youth, the revolutionaries, the militants, and other dropouts from conventional society, the establishment-supporting magazines became passé. They gave up reading these periodicals, their point being that especially the mass magazines had been advocating traditional solutions to the problems disturbing the under-30's and had failed to support, or even to report, dissent. Magazines were regarded as guilty of a lack of openness in their discussions, choosing to ignore rather than face problems. Or they were accused of setting up for their readers false standards and goals—the accumulation of wealth, indifference to social evils, preoccupation with personal comfort and failure to work for the development of the arts, as examples. A substantial number of the under-30's therefore turned to the underground press as their medium of expression.

The "liberated" women or those who wished to be liberated wanted no more articles on how to become beautiful and catch a man. They wanted, instead, expression of their point of view about women's rights. A group of them invaded *The Ladies' Home Journal* offices in 1970 and made their aims clear. Token response came promptly—space for their opinions in a future issue—but later there were more lasting changes. Also, a number of new magazines appeared on the scene, the better known titled *New Woman* and *Ms,* to fulfill what the older ones were charged with failing to do.

A revolution of sorts took place at *Harper's* and the *Atlantic* in both subject matter and writing, in the hope of meeting the demands for greater relevancy. Both these more-than-a-century-old publications made the transition, although it did not come easily at *Harper's* where, when his policies were not welcomed by management, the editor, Willie Morris, resigned. A half dozen staff members followed him in sympathy.

Similarly, changes within the religious world affected the denominational periodicals, one of the larger groups when classified by subject matter. The churches lost many young people because they had turned against organized religion, noting that it, too, tended to support the establishment and countenance wars and other social evils. Felt, also, were the departure from the Roman Catholic church in particular, of many religious, both priests and nuns, as well as the schisms among Southern Baptists and other large bodies over the Indochina War and the rising power of the black race. A direct effect was felt by the religious magazines when the economic stress brought about drops in both circulation and advertising volume, resulting in mergers and the discontinuance of some.

Those periodicals that made only half-hearted attempts at accommodation of their rebellious readers lost face. Some even their lives, as in the case of *The Saturday Evening Post, Look* and *Life,* although the faults in those instances included also managerial errors, the rising costs of production and distribution, and the competition from television for advertising revenue. The *Post* came back in the guise of its more conservative past, hoping to win the support of the older, nostalgic-minded generation. Other media recognized the alienation of youth more forcefully than did magazines which, like newspapers, always have been slow to alter their personalities for, to do so, expensive technical retooling is involved.

One need only scan the titles of articles in the magazines of the late 1960's and early 1970's to note reflections of the new tone in American life which these publications were trying to portray, even though mildly. They echoed a little of the minorities' fight for civil rights, the attack on the problems of poverty, the rise to dominance of soul and rock music, the fad of rather weird drugs, the revolt against certain religious tenets and practices, the concern for the environment, the suspicion of government at any level, the cynicism about war in general and the one in Indochina in particular. Samples:

"A Young Nun's Dangerous Quest for Peace" (*Redbook*); "A Dialogue with My Soledad Son" (*Ebony*); "How the Media Massaged Me" (*Esquire*); "Woman of the Year: Gloria Steinem" (*McCall's*); "Down with Sexist Upbringing" (*Ms*).

The framework for these articles also changed in those years, and is still changing—an alteration was forced by the need for economy. Certain large magazines shrank: *McCall's, Boy's Life, Esquire, Fortune* and *Holiday* dropped from 10½" x 13½" to 8" x 11" in size. This fact may seem to be an incidental detail, but in the magazine world it is a major change. It affects the display of content, for the large and striking photograph is less large and striking on the smaller page. Reading matter also is less impressive, it loses impact. Advertising seems to be larger in relation to editorial matter. But the savings in paper and type composition can be significant. Less paper means less weight also, and that means lower mailing costs.

PROBLEMS WITH MAILING COSTS

Drastic new rate schedules announced since the late 1960's by what now is known as the United States Postal Service have hurt the industry badly. When *Look* ceased in 1971, Gardner Cowles, its founder and board chairman of Cowles Communications, placed part of the blame on the postal rate rises. He further observed: "If recently proposed postage increases go through I predict quite a few tragedies in the next few years." Within 15 months he was proved right: *Life* died.

Before either died, the Postal Service had announced plans to increase by 142 per cent, over a five-year period, the rates for the second class mail—the category in which most magazines are carried. Such a huge jump upward could wipe out, particularly, some magazines of opinion, the arts and religion, already hurt by the necessity to raise subscription rates because of earlier postal policies and the mounting costs of production. Other specialized magazines, such as the small periodicals in the fields of the sciences, education and the law essentially are subscription books, with little or no newsstand distribution and, in view of their specialization or social position, able to command only minimal advertising.

The second class mailing privilege originally was intended to help stimulate public education and discussion as essential elements in a democratic society. Ever since the 1960's this concept seems no longer to be understood in Washington. For example, in defending the rise proposed for 1971, a postal official a year later implied that the publishers' objections obscured the real issues, which he cited as high paper costs, a sluggish economy, falling advertising revenues and new kinds of competition for the print media that created what he called "a financial squeeze"—although such a squeeze has existed for some years.

The postal system is intended as a service to the American people and should no more be considered obligated to make a profit than the fire department of a city or hospitals and schools. Furthermore, the Service announced no plans to add to its revenue in ways not destructive of socially valuable publications. Then, during the politically important year 1972, postal officials announced that the rises might be delayed or abandoned if certain savings could be effected and that an effort also would be made to improve service. These savings were to come from such policies as urging early retirements and not filling nonessential positions. But magazine industry officials were skeptical. They pointed out that the service was so bad that improvement would come easily but that the methods to be used to effect savings would only decrease the efficiency. And this was precisely what happened. Examples of incredible slowness in delivery of first as well as second class mail became more common. Pickups of mail were reduced, further slowing delivery.

CHANGE IN MAGAZINE TYPES

More dramatic than any other has been the actual change in the types of magazines. The general-appeal periodical is on the way out, or at least to limited size in circulation. Gone are the giants: *Collier's, Look, Life, American Weekly, This Week, American, Woman's Home Companion.* Three other equally famous—*The Saturday Evening Post, Liberty* and *Coronet*—also died in recent years, but have been reborn under new ownership. But they have not recovered their status as leaders. At the same time as these occurrences, hundreds of highly specialized periodicals reflecting the new interests and activities of Americans in the 1970's have appeared—dealing with ecology, apartment living and snowmobiling, for instance. (See App. 4.)

As a further result of changes in public taste and standards are more freedom of expression and wider latitude in choice of subject matter.

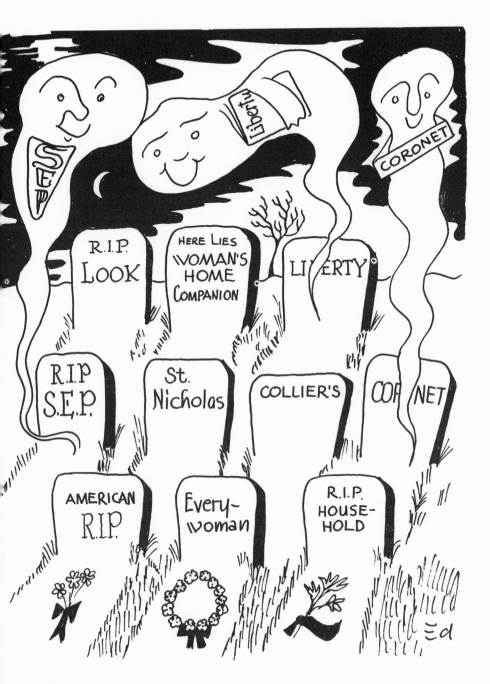

Cartoon by Edmund C. Arnold.

Readers, however, continue to approve or object to what is between magazine covers, and by their support or neglect can control a publication's future. Intellectual currents also bring changes in magazines. Because it went counter to the views of many of its readers on the Vietnam war in the 1960's, *The Reporter,* for example, lost the support of some important intellectual leaders among whom were numerous contributors. On the other hand, subscriptions and contributions shifted to publications whose views coincided with the opinions of those leaders. A notable instance is the *New York Review of Books.*

Such shifts occur not only because of viewpoints. They are also brought about by the forces reflecting interest in content. The purely literary magazines, as well as those that shared their space with literature, have had to make more room for non-fiction. Such journalistic material as editorials, articles, reviews and essays dealing with current social and political problems fill the gaps left by poems and short stories. The mortality among the literary magazines, as a result, was great. Economically feeble as many always are, they succumbed more easily under the new pressures. A major loss was *Kenyon Review,* for 31 years a leading literary quarterly. The underground press gained some of the readers lost by the literary publications. Academic people, scientists and others considered as the "intellectual class" have come out of their ivory towers as never before. Their choices of reading have done much to change the nature of those influential magazines aimed, not at the masses, but at an intellectual élite. (See App. 7.)

ORIENTATION TO PEOPLE

Preoccupation with people is a long-term trend that has reached a higher point than ever before in the 1970's. It, too, is a force for change in magazines that has been active for at least a century. It was not so much a preoccupation in earlier times as a recognition that material about people is a guarantee of reader interest. In its early manifestations there were biographical articles paying honor to noted writers, artists, religious, governmental or military figures. Typical was an article in *Harper's Monthly* during its first year, 1850: "Thomas Carlyle" was the undramatic title chosen by the author, George Gilfellan. In the *Democratic Review* for the some year unsigned pieces appeared about Jenny Lind, Edmund Burke, Leigh Hunt, Edgar Allan Poe, Mirabeau, Lord Chesterfield and a half dozen now forgotten politicians.

Attention to people was intensified with the arrival of a new century—ranging from the successful industrialists such as Henry Frick, the glamorout singers like Lillian Russell, to the notable actors such as the Barrymore family. After a time sports heroes, popular entertainers from vaudeville and the movies joined the group. Soon whole magazines were devoted to cinema stars, giving rise to a flood of fan magazines; some of the original periodicals still exist but now cover television and radio personalities as well. In our time, every conceivable public figure, including criminals, is a part of the cult of personality which has affected the content of most magazines, including those devoted to special areas. So absorbed are editors in people, knowing that readers respond to people, that the stories of even "little people" are being told increasingly. The nation in general is becoming more aware of such minority groups as American Indians, Mexican-Americans and Afro-Americans, thanks at least in small part to periodicals.

This tendency has been aided by absorption of other media in human beings, for newspapers, radio programs, telecasts and books also are people-oriented. Another factor is the journalistic view, strengthened by the works of such readability specialists as Robert Gunning and Rudolf Flesch, who make the point that the way to catch readers' attention is to make people the "heroes," instead of abstract ideas. Thus *The New Yorker* will build the story of some activity around a typical person rather than emphasize the activity of such. *Ebony* will depend upon pictures, but they are of people rather than things.

NEWS COVERAGE

The nature of the news today has made changes in magazines also. Events are so numerous, so frequent, so fast-moving and so complex that more magazines than ever make room at least for its interpretation, and many even provide first-hand reporting. News coverage is changing in magazines that carry it, and is a function of many more periodicals than readers usually realize, for not only do the majority print news but they also present it in substantial quantity. Three newsmagazines are all that come to many readers' minds when news in magazines is mentioned. In reality magazines with news content run into the thousands. More than 2,300 trade, technical and business magazines print it, as do hundreds of educational, sports, scientific and other special-subject books. *Business Week* and *Sports Illustrated,* both with large circulations, are built almost entirely upon news, for instance.

Time, Newsweek and *U.S. News and World Report,* now well established, have been riding to success on the new place that news occupies in American life and, in turn, have influenced other magazines to spare more room for coverage of timely events.

The picturization of the news on television has been a force for change, too, as has the spread of photojournalism. All the media have become more news-conscious by the pressure of enormously important events—new wars and continuation of old ones, scientific experiments and discoveries (particularly space travel), business fluctuations, international agreements on trade and currency, international crises over oil supplies and ocean fishing, and aircraft hijackings are among the more obvious examples.

Thus we now see even consumer magazines, such as those intended for housewives, carrying "newsflash" pages on developments of special interest to their readers, noting for them changes in government regulations of food packaging or content and similar news. General magazines like *Parade* and other inserts in newspapers in similar format have found such news-letter-like pages highly popular with readers. The presence of so much news in magazines should help to change the concept of periodicals from that of being largely for entertainment.

THE "NEW JOURNALISM"

The New Journalism, a vague term to describe what is thought to be a new approach in writing, is another force for change that has affected directly several important magazines and indirectly scores of others. But its newness is currently contested as is its quality. Ted Solotaroff, editor of *The American Review,* sees cant in the new journalism, which he has described as "2 parts low down, 1 part corn, and a dash of obscenity." At its best, this new journalism aims to accomplish its purpose by applying fictional techniques to non-fiction. Actual conversations are introduced as a novelist or short story writer would use invented dialogue, for example. But some of its exponents identify it with what is called subjective, advocracy or alternative writing, whereby the writer injects his own reactions and views at length and gives them the importance of other parts of his material. No pretense is made of objectivity. The so-called underground press has used this approach heavily.

Leading practitioners of the new journalism include Jimmy Breslin, Joan Dideon, Dan Wakefield, Gloria Steinem, Norman Mailer, Truman Capote, Gay Talese and the later Tom Wolfe. Wolfe at first used an apparently hysterical writing style in which punctuation and capitalization of words ran wild. His eccentric book titles (the books themselves compiled from his magazine writings), set the tone—*Electric Kool-Aid Acid Test* and *The Kandy-Colored Tangerine Flake Streamline Baby,* for instance. But it was not so much individual style eccentricities as attitude and point of view that were picked up by the magazines and great numbers of the undergrounds. Wolfe's attack upon *The New Yorker* in 1965, in the newspaper supplement to the New York *Herald Tribune* that was the matrix for the present *New York* magazine, although filled with errors, may have moved the older magazine to some mild changes.

Other magazines than *New York* have availed themselves of this freedom for their contributors, notably *Esquire, Harper's* and *Ramparts.* But the relaxed, casual tone of this genre of writing is encountered now and then in periodicals whose editors welcome it as a refreshing style giving variety to the publication. *Time* and *Newsweek* not only have kept an eye on the new journalism development but also printed some of it. Naturally it has found its way into some of the newer magazines, such as *New Woman* during its first year before it was suspended for re-formulating, and in *Ms.*

SELLING BY-PRODUCTS

The growing trend to use magazines as salesmen for by-products affects their management as well as their content. Managements now sometimes approach publishing with a purpose far different than the traditional. If one riffles through magazines of two decades ago the change is clear. Today the aim of some managements is not primarily to serve the public by providing a forum, conveying new literature or transmitting information. They do not even pretend that the main goal is to make money directly from magazine subscriptions, single copy sales and advertising revenue: an accepted, traditional purpose. Their new aim is to build a mailing list for a mail order business that will benefit the manufacturers of certain products, often the very firm that publishes the magazine.

Stephen Isaacs, of the Washington *Post* staff, in a four-part study of present-day magazines published in 1972, observed that certain publishers are "making more by selling by-products through their magazines than they are from the magazines." In listing some of those by-products Isaacs noted that the company which owns *Playboy* now promotes in its pages its clubs, hotels, glasses and cuff-links, among many more enterprises and products which it also owns.

Related in more detail in a later chapter is the instance of the CRM Corp. which, when it became owner of *Saturday Review,* began this process of using the magazine as a vehicle for sales of other products or services (books, a book club and other magazines published by the same firm), a policy that led to the resignation, in disagreement, of the magazine's noted editor, Norman Cousins.

All this is not to say that every magazine in America is reflecting the social, moral and cultural changes manifested during the past few years. Most readers rebel against changes, others suffer it grudgingly, a few welcome it. The thousands of business journals have remained essentially unaltered. They may have had face-liftings in typography and over-all graphic design but basically they reflect only what has varied in the particular specialties they represent. Such magazines serve their own tight little worlds. What their readers demand they also respond to, but the demand is essentially the same—news of special interests not available elsewhere, reports of developments, experiences and experiments in the field and warnings about impending government activities that may affect such interests.

But it is the reader who is the key, no matter what the magazine. How well do these readers know their magazines? What do they know about the workings of their magazines? What are their attitudes? Such questions should be examined if readers are to be understood and themselves are to understand.

2

The Readers Six

Either I, or magazines, have changed. An hour spent with most of them now leaves me with exhausted patience, a queasy stomach, positive symptoms of a couple of ailments I didn't know existed and a general feeling of irritation.

Thus Mrs. Betty Volk, a Cleveland *Press* columnist, asking in her paper for magazines to return to the days when they made their readers—or at least Mrs. Volk—comfortable. She used to enjoy them, and did so "curled up in a comfortable chair with a good light." Somebody, she advised, should start "publishing a comfortable magazine."

Mrs. Volk represents one of more than a half-dozen types of people who respond in one way or another to magazines. She is of The Discomfitted Group. The most important other readers are The Mistrustful, The Annoyed, The Bewildered, The Indifferent, and The Satisfied. The Ignorers represent another kind of reaction. Obviously not all readers fall into the first six categories. Other types, less numerous, also cast eyes over magazine pages. Still others ignore periodicals in their own peculiar ways, such as using them as drawer liners, door stops or plugs for basement leaks. Most read their magazines from front to back, but a good number start at the stern, apparently bracing themselves for the heavier cargo to be encountered near the prow. Then there are those readers who use magazines as sleep inducers, as soporifics—or as extensions of their own personalities or propagandas. For magazine readers are a diverse group of beings with varying ways of responding to this form of journalism.

Digging below the topsoil of reactions reveals that the responses are directed largely at what is known in the publishing business as consumer magazines. The legendary man on the street speaks as if those of general aim are the only ones deserving to be called magazines. Possibly that is a natural view, for even some scholars of the nation's journalism equate the word *magazine* only with the mass circulation publications of broad appeal.

15

They never agree, however, about what to call the journalism left over, although it looks like magazines. Mrs. Volk, for instance, wrote of spending an hour "with most of them." Just what she means by reading is not clear, but if she even as much as glanced at everything in the popular magazines of recent years it would take her innumerable hours. And she apparently overlooks the thousands catering to special interests.

THE DISCOMFITTED READER

Mrs. Volk and the other Discomfitted Readers are unhappy because they no longer can so easily use magazines as a way of escape from life's realities. Or, to put it another way, in recent years numerous periodicals, even some of the most specialized, have broadened their bases and, as is inevitable, discomfitted some readers and gained the loyalty of others.

The loss of cheeriness—or what was considered cheeriness a quarter of a century or more ago—that has saddened and upset some readers results not only from the kinds of material published but also from the way that material is treated. As Mrs. Volk lamented, the magazines she reads deal heavily with various aspects of sex and health. So do many others she may not read; in fact, these two subjects have given birth in recent years to new magazines although others have been in the field for some time: *Sexual Behavior* and *Family Health* are among the newcomers. In 1970 and 1971 a magazine of limited popularity, *Harper's,* offended some readers by the frank language of certain contributors, particularly Norman Mailer. In other publications the coarseness or candor is less obvious, hidden under sociological jargon. At *Harper's,* commonly considered a periodical concerned with important public affairs, the management objected not particularly or at least not openly to the clinical details about women's sexual liberation but to the loss of advertising revenue and of circulation—these losses having resulted from inept editing, including too many one-subject issues of limited appeal or method of treatment.

Four-letter words, at least those that once were represented by Ernest Hemingway's device of writing *obscenity* in their place, or by blank lines, asterisks or partial lines, are not the only sources of discomfort for readers who turn to magazines for surcease from anxiety. Other sources that disturb are the space allotted to writers who call for social reform, even revolution, and the reactions of some periodicals to those calls. Merely reporting the events of the day even if only by photographs can provoke distress. Portrayals of ghetto conditions, campus rebels in action, war scenes, strikes and lockouts, and trials of dissenters do not produce satisfied smiles from readers hankering for the quieter days of escape fiction and medical articles concerning nothing more sexy than the hives.

To make matters still worse for The Discomfitted, some magazines venture beyond reporting what is happening. They can be found cheering

"Hot ziggetty! 'Liberty'!"

Drawing by Modell;
© 1971 *The New Yorker* Magazine, Inc.

revolutionaries on. Frightening indeed to the Pollyannas of the day are the contents of the "underground" magazines (not all undergrounds are newspapers; even some of those that look like newspapers turn out really to be magazines in content). Thus the muckraking group, such as *Ramparts, The Realist, Evergreen* and, while it lasted, *Scanlan's,* are upsetting. *Scanlan's,* just before it declared itself in bankruptcy in 1971, printed instructions for making explosive devices useful in blowing up buildings.

Other readers in this group are made miserable by another type of content. A reader in Oregon wrote to *Holiday* in 1969:

> Your editorial policy disturbs me.
> We live in time of strife and acute human problems, and while it is not the function of an entertainment magazine to propose solutions, it is also not its function to compound the problems. In my opinion, the Hedonistic, amoral approach *Holiday* seems to be taking will do just that.

The letters editor printed over it: "Don't Make Waves." Whether a magazine should make waves—which usually means another cliché, don't

rock the boat—will be examined later. Making waves of any sort disturbs
the comfortable readers. They were given an opportunity to return to a
happier magazine past in the 1970's, when *Liberty,* a weekly, was repub-
lished as a quarterly, subtitled "the Nostalgia Magazine," with most of it
resembling the issues of 1924–1950. *The Saturday Evening Post* was revived, also as a quarterly, full of wistful cartoons, stories, and articles from
rosier days when it was a weekly. About the same time someone issued, for
newsstand sale only, an anthology of the old humor magazine, *Life,* the
one Henry Luce bought so he could use its title on his then new picture
book.

THE MISTRUSTFUL READER

The Mistrustful Reader is not agitated in his soul because his peace of
mind is disturbed. No. He is the cynic, more upset in his social conscience
than in his pocketbook. It bothers him to find in his mail, as he does many
times a year, subscription offers. They are for new subscribers only (10
months for $2.99, whereas he pays $6 to $8 for 12). He, however, has
been a subscriber to *Like* or *Stare* or whatever it may be for 15 years and
gets no reward for his long loyalty; he paid the regular price for all his
renewals.

All this treatment is bad enough. What really makes him suspicious
of the honesty of the magazine business is what he considers the deceptions
that occur when a subscription sales crew hits town.

The attitude of mistrust began, in all likelihood, when some years
back his front-door bell was rung one Saturday afternoon. On the porch
stood a young man on crutches. He was there, he said, representing an
Institute of Something or Other. Could he have a minute to explain its
non-profit purpose? He was invited in, even offered coffee. It was not long
before the Institute turned out to be nothing more than a cover for selling
subscriptions to various national magazines. The Instituter was a most
appealing young fellow. He actually needed those crutches and the points a
long-term subscription could give him. Mr. (or Ms.) Mistrustful Reader
subscribed—and waited months before complaining that he never received
the magazines he'd ordered and paid for in advance. Finally they came.

After that first visit there were more. There came youths of either sex
needing credits toward a college scholarship or votes with which to open a
business of their own in some part of a distant city where the underprivileged live. Their approach was indirect. The situation was well portrayed by Bob Barnes, the cartoonist. He showed a housewife saying to the
young woman on her porch: "As I understand it, you're taking a poll for
the Academy of Social and Intellectual Development . . . That's very
fascinating, but I don't want any magazine subscriptions."

When M.R. read that some of the big companies were in trouble with the Federal Trade Commission over their subscription-selling methods, he felt vindicated in his growing mistrustfulness. More than ever suspicious, he concluded that greedy publishers use such methods to exploit the physically handicapped. He was further dismayed, in 1972, to read that *Life* was fooled by Clifford Irving with his alleged biography of Howard Hughes despite Time Inc.'s highly touted system of checking its magazines' copy before publication.

Some Mistrustful Readers' social consciousness also expresses itself in traditional conservative or liberal patriotism, if such pigeon-holing words can be said to mean anything these days. The traditional patriot writes letters like this one:

> For some time I have been dissatisfied with *SR*'s extremist left stand, but the final straw was the so-called review by Henry S. Resnik in the Dec. 12 issue of four books dealing with the Chicago riot trial. This was a piece of propaganda aimed, like the books themselves and the actions of the rioters, toward the establishment of a leftist totalitarian dictatorship in the United States.

The *Saturday Review* did not let the complaint go unanswered. It headed the letter simply "Propaganda," but an editor's note said:

> Precisely because *SR* believes in a democratic marketplace of ideas, its critics are permitted to voice their own opinions even when they conflict with those of the editors.

To the editor of *The American Way,* an airline magazine—the colorful type of periodical that sticks from the pocket on the seat in front of each passenger—came a letter from an Arizona businessman who declared:

> You should seriously consider changing your magazine . . . It is too liberal, atheistic, and communistic. Your July edition had nothing about America and its independence and forefathers! I did not like the psychedelic pictures; Hawaii isn't like that! Mark Twain was an agnostic! Either change or expect to be changed!

The editor made no comment except what was implied in the heading, which was ". . . Or Else."

The liberal patriot, by comparison, rarely writes to the major magazines to complain about their conservatism. He is more given to boycotting them. *Time* and *Playboy* have aroused such boycotts. Opie, the cartoonist, in a *New Yorker* drawing published during the late 1950's, echoed the boycott attitude. His picture shows two men and a woman, all young, at a coffee shop table. Says the girl to an indignant-looking man: "But Lester, is it not enough just being against everything that *Time* magazine is for?" A year or so later the same magazine carried another cartoon, also of a restaurant scene, in which a severe-looking waiter informs a man holding *Time* conspicuously as he reads it that he is "afraid we must ask you to leave." The boycotts against *Playboy* have come from members of women's liberation groups, who insist that the magazine exploits women in its drawings and prose alike.

The patriotic Mistrustful Reader, whatever the hue or position on the political spectrum, is concerned not because the magazines he reads deal with current issues but because of the views they hold. That, at least, is what he tells himself. In fact, he would be happy if only his view or none at all were presented.

THE ANNOYED READER

Although the Annoyed Reader is not bothered much by unethical selling practices or distasteful political views, he is indeed irritated by certain less obvious behavior, especially if he is a businessman who must go through a dozen or more specialized magazines that serve his industrial or financial interests. The coupons to be cut out of advertising, the other cardboardy pieces of paper that pop up at him as he turns pages, the island advertisements (these are small ads stuck into the midst of an article or short story and surrounded not by water but reading matter), and the pages of apparent editorial prose that really is disguised advertising—these all annoy.

His wife tells him one day about the grocery store cashier in a Louisiana town who bought the leftover issues of *Family Circle* and clipped all its coupons. They saved her more money than the magazines had cost her. But these flapping pieces of paper intrude on reading, just the same, and they bother him. And his wife. Annoyance also sets in for each of them when either must hunt for the continuation of a story or article in the wilderness of advertising at the back. And, if as happens now and then, the number in the "Please turn to Page . . ." line is wrong, you can hear "Damn this magazine!"

Not the kind really to become inflamed about such matters, the Annoyed Reader nevertheless does want to know when he is supposed to be reading paid advertising and when the material is what the editor (not the business department) intended for him. In his specialized publications he now and then comes across what looks like an article but up in the corner, almost unnoticeable, is the word "Advertisement." If he used such language as "typographical dress" he would say that such material is in the same t.d. as something written by a staff person or free lancer for the editorial department and therefore is disguised advertising. He may have read, several years back, of the instance when *Reader's Digest,* presumably inadvertently, lost or dropped the warning word on many reprints of a certain advertisement that had been set in type to look exactly like a *Digest* article.

Yet Mr. Annoyed is not bothered enough by these practices to write publishing houses about them. He is too sophisticated or cynical about that. Instead he writes about content that piques him. There was the letter by a one-time reader who said he had given up the magazine because it published the work of only one writer on a certain subject and failed to give the viewpoints of many others who could contribute. But if, as he said, "he seldom read" the magazine anyway, how did he know this to be so? His superiority got the better of him, that time.

THE BEWILDERED READER

The Bewildered Reader, on the other hand, is unsophisticated, even naive. Or perhaps only puzzled. His head spins as he passes a big magazine stand or as he reads about the births and deaths of periodicals in the press columns of the newsmagazines. Like the school kid who cannot understand math or physics, he fails to fathom the rapidly changing world of publishing and journalism. Chances are that some of the new magazines out in January will be gone by June; few go on and some of the apparent successes fade away before many years, even though there are reports of net gains. The situation puzzles him.

One night at a dinner he meets a man in the magazine business. "Whatever became of . . . ?" he asks, and reels off some name like *Clyde* or *Realm* or *Huè* or *Venture* or *Eye* or *Jock.* He is not sure whether the *Post* really is back or if the *Companion* of today has anything to do with the famous old *Woman's Home Companion* he used to see at his grandmother's home when he was a child. He reads rumors about the troubles besetting *Life* and then its obituary. But he also sees the ads of publishers proclaiming that all is well, that advertising is picking up this quarter or circulation climbing steeply this half. He has read of troubles at *Vogue* or *Harper's Bazaar* or *Essence,* mostly staff changes.

Another Bewildered Reader sees advertisements for so many new magazines she cannot believe that the publishing industry is having any financial troubles. She recalls seeing somewhere that Time Inc. dismissed or did not refill jobs of 15% of its employes during a recent year. Yet she hears about or sees many new titles, some of direct interest to her, such as *MS, Modern Woman, New Woman, Girl Talk.* Her husband backs her up, for he has read about several large companies planning from two to four new magazines. And around the city he has noticed *National Lampoon, Black Sports, On the Sound, On the Shore.* How come they appear if times are so hard for magazines?

The essence of the bewilderment is in the expression, "What's going on here, anyway?" It is uttered in the hope that somebody knows. As the American magazine industry stood in the early 1970's it is not certain anyone really knew. As in any other business, the experts disagree. Henry R. Luce provided the historic example when, in the depression year 1930, just as the market crashed in fact, he started *Fortune*. Subscriptions cost $10 a year each, then a fabulous figure. And it continues, albeit a bit unsteadily, more than four decades later. With the newsstands crowded with colorful magazines for all male tastes, Hugh Hefner in 1953 launched a rival for *Esquire* called *Playboy,* deliberately not dating the first issue. For how did he know he could bring out a second the next month? Twenty years later it had reached seven million circulation, at a dollar a copy, and was fat with high-priced advertising; it also had become part of a huge entertainment empire consisting of clubs and hotels. It may be that with the bravado of gamblers at the races or players of the numbers game publishers start new magazines. If readers knew the risks of such enterprises they might not invest in any of the few that are public companies, but then neither do they know the risks in many other firms so dependent upon the public. Or they might do more to support the new magazines they like, whatever the form of ownership and management. Since they do not know, they naturally wonder about the quick comings and goings.

THE INDIFFERENT READER

The Indifferent Reader is not upset by magazine sins of omission or commission where social issues are concerned. Magazines, to him, are neither textbooks nor opinion-makers. They are sources of entertainment or symbols of prestige, not to be taken too seriously but convenient to fill in the time when there's nothing of interest on television. Such readers like *Saturday Review, The New Yorker* or *Esquire* for its cartoons, *National Geographic* for its photographs, *Playboy* or *Cosmopolitan* for its pin-ups. They are bored by the deep thinkers who contribute the articles that run between the cartoons and by the literary fare—the formless poetry and the sad, sad short stories—run in and out of glamorous advertising. They are among the readers, also, who like to study the pictures in the high fashion magazines, *Vogue* and *Harper's Bazaar,* or the less fancy *Lady's Circle* and *Glamour.* Some of the Indifferent intend some day to read those serious articles but never get to them; the issues pile up and then are thrown out.

Large sums are spent by the Indifferent for handsome bookazines or magabooks, such as *Horizon* or *American Heritage,* but they serve more as decorations than as reading matter in certain houses. These adless, erudite and bound-like-books periodicals are too attractive to throw in the discard pile for the Salvation Army pick-up truck. The Indifferent Reader eventually gives them to a nearby library or to some artistic or scholarly friend who appreciates them. A few, including *The American Gun* and *Eros,* last longer for other than aesthetic reasons: fun to look at by sex or shooting hobbyists. But if they were stolen some night it is unlikely that money would be spent recovering or replacing them. The readers just do not care that much. They can get along. New issues will provide the pastime opportunities that magazines still represent.

THE SATISFIED READER

Editors and advertising directors of the larger publications spend money to find out who their readers are. They send out questionnaires or print them in issues, offering rewards for responses. Or they send interviewers to selected subscribers' homes or hire research firms to provide what in the business is called "reader profiles." In the process they learn the annual income, the educational background, the extent of property ownership, family size and other statistics. What is even more important, at least to the advertising department, they find out how many cars, snowmobiles, TV sets, frigs and other pieces of machinery are owned and what use is made, if any, of toothpaste, shampoos, cake mixes and mustard, among other scores of commodities as well as services like insurance and banking.

Judging by the results of such probing, most magazine readers are not

Cartoon by Edmund C. Arnold.

Cartoon by Edmund C. Arnold.

the meanies who complain and gripe or, worst of all, who fail to renew all subscriptions and flee to the underground press. They are reasonably well satisfied, like the Rochester housewife who wrote one of the papers in that part of New York state that she is "an avid reader" of women's magazines. "In fact," she confessed, "I practically devour them."

She described her method, which is first to give "a quick skimming of the entire journal as soon as I bring it from the mailbox; later, a careful reading from cover to cover." She admitted, however, that the homemaking advice did not always work out perfectly but this was only a mild complaint.

The Satisfied Reader, like that Rochestrian, is a real enthusiast, one who warms a staff members's heart by his or her loyalty. Such satisfaction is most vocal when a club has an editor as its speaker on some special occasion. Inevitably, after the question-and-answer period, a number of admirers of his publication seek him out to tell him that they read every issue and have done so for years, or that they own every number published, including the first. (The leaning piles may be in the cellar or attic and never looked at from one year to the next, but there they are, to be sure.) And the older and larger the periodical the more such pleased readers.

Among the most devoted of *aficionados* are those of the *National Geo-graphic, Reader's Digest, Fortune, Arizona Highways, Horizon* and *Holiday,* which are not too specialized. If only the readers of such early periodicals as *The Columbian* and *The Port-Folio* had been thus faithful; it would not be so difficult now to find copies in good condition.

The most satisfied readers are those who subscribe to or buy at news-stands magazines catering to their special interests. Although it does not last into adulthood, usually such loyalty is possessed by youngsters who cherish comic magazines. Theirs is a fidelity to a group whose members pass from hand to hand or are exchanged in great clusters. Such multiple exposure would delight Time Inc., the Meredith Publishing Company and a dozen other big firms that rejoice to announce that they have such and such a number of pass-along readers. But their clusters are small by com-parison. Next, perhaps, are the hobbyists, like the numismatists, philatelists, photographers and antique hounds. They really read intensively in their *Coins, Stamps, Popular Photography* and *Antiques,* and save all issues for future reference, some even loyally buying binders in which to protect them. Scientists and scholars, although they are too few in number to support their magazines to the extent that they become affluent, also are loyal readers, since they obviously need them to keep abreast of their professions. Yet they are not 100 per cent satisfied; they are given to complain about the cost of memberships and the irrelevancy of some content.

One important type of reaction to magazines infrequently dealt with is that from the Ignorers, who are not readers at all. They usually are the ex-readers or non-readers who no longer even skim or riffle. They depend upon television, radio or paperback books. Or they spurn the printed word altogether. Such response often comes from among members of what is called nowadays the turned-off generation. They rely—if they see print except on food packages—on the underground press for their chief jour-nalistic printed fare. Many of these several hundred publications actually contain little but magazine material, however: essays attacking sexists, historical articles recounting the origin and development of some revolu-tionary faction, personal experiences of readers engaged in community action, and a modicum of news.

The Ignorers are in effect voting "no confidence" in the social order of which most magazines in America are a reflection. But the rest of the population, the great bulk of periodical readers, is not interested in dis-connecting from the order itself, and continues to read, skeptically or acceptingly.

Diversity, therefore, is characteristic of the body of magazine readers. It also is a reflection of the extraordinary and confusing variety of the magazine world itself, of which most persons who use periodicals may be unaware.

3

The
Diversity of Magazines

MANY MECHANICAL AND SCIENTIFIC WONDERS were displayed at the Chicago World's Fair of the early 1930's, but the attraction that drew magazine buffs was a building housing Time Inc.'s display. For here were 2,000 different periodicals, most of them popular or influential in their circles, from the various countries served by Time Inc.'s own output. Arranged in long racks, they comprised an overwhelming display. Yet it was only a small part of the magazine journalism available, even in the U.S.A., which publishes an estimated 20,000, many times more than any other country.

If such an exhibit were prepared today it might reflect the intense specialization of knowledge at this time in world history. Magazines are almost as diverse as their readers, seemingly several for every human enterprise. No one has made an absolute check on the exact extent; it would be incorrect the day released, so many come and go. Our interests and activities change rapidly, and new magazines appear quickly to satisfy demand or for which publishers estimate there may be a need.

Some realization of this diversity may come by noting only a few titles current as this book is being written—all are U.S. periodicals:

Bachhus Journal	*Meat*	*Afternoon TV*
Exceptional Parent	*RN*	*National Future*
Hot Rod	*Skating*	*Farmer*
Biscuit and	*Surfer*	*Current Audio*
Cracker Maker	*Woman Golfer*	*Scripts*
Volume Feeding	*Pool and Patio*	*Juris Doctor*
Our Dumb Animals	*Hunting Dog*	*Natural Life Styles*
Italamerican	*Oral Hygiene*	*Skin Diver*
Black Business Digest	*Auto Glass Journal*	*Body Fashions*

Hundreds of others could be named, some even more specialized than these. Well over half of the 20,000 different magazines relate to the business world, about 9,000 being what are known as "house publications." About 2,300 more are such trade journals as books devoted to, for example, the hardware business. The other nearly 9,000 include those best known to the general reader—the consumer magazines that occupy the prominent places on the newsstands or are in the tallest stacks—as well as the thousands devoted to various broad interests in the realms of sports, fashion, travel, television and scores of other such subjects.

Furthermore, they have all the known frequencies—from daily to annual, with weekly and monthly the most common. Sizes also give them wide variety, with *Vogue* at one extreme, so large as to be cumbersome, and pocket-size at the other, as typified by *Jet* or *Science Digest*. In between are other dimensions. Thickness, different types of paper, ranges of color in the paper or laid on it by printing, special covers or none, varying kinds of binding and mixtures of reproduction methods all contribute to the diversity. Newspapers are more or less standardized in all these matters, but magazines still display individuality. (See App. 1.)

Defining the Magazine

Content is a jungle of reading matter. Much more so than in any other medium, anything goes and everything is there when our magazines are all put together—as they might be if displayed in some enormous aircraft hangar capable of mounting them separately on racks, *à la* that Time Inc. exhibit. Over the years only books have offered the varieties of treatment and style that now can be found in magazines. Today, not only can the reader find a magazine on almost any subject entrancing him but also it is likely that he can find it written or illustrated in a way most agreeable to him. With some exceptions, sports magazines are couched in the jargon of each game, just as the underground political magazines spout the language of Marx, Mao, Lenin and Ché—translated, to be sure. The lovers of pornography now have their pick, including pictures, in magazine form. And the pundits have scores of journals whose vocabulary is practically gibberish to others.

But no one has that problem with newspapers. They look and sound alike from Miami to Southern California and from Oregon to Maine. Dozens may be owned by one firm, and reflect that fact. And hundreds buy the same comic strips, columns and other features. The traveler from the hometown need never be homesick for his local daily, for he can find much of the content at the next corner drug store—it is called the *Journal* instead of the *News,* perhaps, but that's no matter because the viewpoints and many of the same fixed content are there.

Such standardization is not true, however, of magazines. Consequently there is no such animal as a "typical" magazine. Nor is it possible, accurately writing, to use the word *magazines*—as is done in this book and all others about the business—as if all 20,000 were more or less alike. But one has to continue using the term, because otherwise a writer would constantly be calling attention to the exceptions. The periodical world is complex in its own way. Not only is it the largest medium of communication in the U.S.A. in number of units but the magazine is the most advanced in technology, capable of achieving printed effects repeatedly and regularly, all at extraordinary speed.

What, then, is this unstandardized product of the press, the magazine? Just about anything any of us want to call it. Once it was defined by its physical appearance. That great scholar of the American press, Frank Luther Mott, worded a long-used definition in which he specified that the publication be *bound*. He also indicated that the content be *general*. Not long ago, however, Julien Elfenbein, another analyst of the magazine world—although more concerned about the business periodical than any other because that was the type he edited for several decades—expressed the view that how the publication is *bound* is irrelevant and that what counts is what it *contains*. In short, that format is unimportant. If Elfenbein's view is acceptable, it opens the magazines' door to several thousand more publications often thought of as newspapers—such as most members of the underground press and many examples of overground political, labor, education and entertainment press products, to mention just a few areas served by periodicals that look like newspapers but actually have magazine content.

Readers care nothing, of course, for definitions and classifications and categories. And why should they? What they want are the words and pictures. To the annoyance of scholars they ignore careful distinctions; the surveys indicate that readers rarely think of a specialized publication, dubbed something like *The American Soft Drink Journal* or *The Humble Way,* as a magazine. Say they: a magazine is a publication one can buy easily from a newsstand, more or less as one can pick up *Good Housekeeping* or *True.* Such fancy periodicals as *Dance Perspectives* or *American Heritage* are something else again. Just what certain publications are that make masses of readers slight them is not clear. One hears people refer to *TV Guide* as "that little magazine with the programs in it" (as if it were some minor effort of a local newspaper) not realizing that "that little magazine" sells 17 million copies every week, carries influential editorials and articles that flank each side of the program section, and cuts considerable ice in the industry. At least they call it a magazine, even though they do not seem to equate it with others.

Between the wide variety of magazines and the insistence of the public

Cartoon by Edmund C. Arnold.

that the consumer type is the only publication that deserves the name, therefore, it is not easy to make meaningful generalizations.

NEWSMAGAZINES

Perhaps, then, readers of this book will accept as a member of the magazine family a publication whose content is not predominantly spot news yet tries, through articles and pictures and perhaps some fiction, to view news matters at longer range than do newspapers. Or at least most newspapers, for one always must make exceptions of such dailies as the *Christian Science Monitor* and the New York *Times*. But what of the newsmagazines? To begin with, they contain more than news. Furthermore, what news they print hardly is timely; most of it was known days before a particular issue of *Newsweek, Jet* or *Business Week* was printed—it was on radio and television and in the newspapers. People buy such periodicals as a convenience, to confirm the electronic media and to see how the story is told, to discover what, if anything, they missed or was missed by the other media, to see the story in a different perspective, to see relationships and meanings impossible to discern from day-to-day coverage, or for the records they provide. What, also of the trade journal, such as *Modern Beauty Shop?* Is not such a magazine full of news, news the ordinary citizen does not know? True. But it is not intended for the ordinary citizen. Much of its news is aimed at the supermarket managers or others related to the operation of such stores, at the people who run hairdressing salons, or those who are engaged in doing dry cleaning. These people get some of the same news from other specialized periodicals, from industry news letters and publicity releases, from the business sections of daily papers and from their association publications. What they also value are the special articles which are not news but true magazine material, such as reports on the changing buying power and habits of geographic, demographic and ethnic groups of citizens.

MAGAZINES AND NEWSPAPERS COMPARED

Such diversity (the serious scholars prefer to call it multifariousness) comes about because of two forces: competition between media and the method of producing magazines.

From its beginnings in this country, some years after the first periodical was published in 1741, the magazine was essentially a regional, even a national, publication. The newspaper, whose history goes back about 50 years more, on the other hand, has remained mainly local in distribution. In fact, the United States, unlike most other nations, has no national newspaper—not even the New York *Times* qualifying, although perhaps it comes closer than any other. The country still is too large for a newspaper to reach all parts of it even on the same day, in depth. And no weekly has made much of a dent although the effort continues, as witness the *National Observer.* But the magazines, coming out less frequently and making little pretense at carrying spot news, have managed far better to gain national acceptance, outstripping the most widely bought papers many times over.

The Reader's Digest, early in the 1970's, had about 18 million circulation a month in the U.S.A. alone, to which 10 million more were added for its foreign editions. *TV Guide* had 17 million, *Parade* 12 million, *Better Homes* nearly 8 million, *National Geographic* in excess of 6 million. In fact, more than 60 magazines have a million or more circulation for each issue on the annual average whereas only four U.S. newspapers exceed a million, the largest being the New York *Daily News* which on Sundays reaches 3 million. Both newspapers and magazines, especially the general consumer periodicals, have multiple reading of each copy. This takes place in beauty parlors, doctors' offices, libraries, and includes the tightwads who read free as they stand at news kiosks or in front of the supermarket racks. Such reading of each copy by more than one person spreads a magazine's ideas, enhances the power of its advertising and makes friends who may become subscribers. But none of this makes the newspapers as national in scope and influence as magazines, for thousands of the latter keep the whole country in focus for most of their content. Clearly regional books, like *Philadelphia* or *San Francisco*, are not, of course, aimed at readers everywhere. Nor can most periodicals for employees, often called internal organs, stray from home territory in their subject matter. (See App. 12, 13.)

INDIVIDUALITY IN FORMAT

Yet magazines are not easily mistaken for one another because considerable individuality exists among them, thanks often to their art directors. To be sure, certain major periodicals have their imitators, but most imitations have failed. One may at a glance mistake *Essence* for *Redbook,* especially since black faces no longer are a novelty on women's magazine covers. Each is a leader in its own field. But after all, there is only one *New Yorker,* one *Wisdom,* one *Audience,* one *Sports Illustrated.* No one ever would mistake *True* for *Fortune* or *Harper's Bazaar* for *The Woman.* Neither of these resembles *Current History* or *Playboy* and certainly not *Black Belt.* Competition has driven them to adopt their own personalities and, in turn, has produced distinctive graphics in which all the variations possible with design, typography and printing are brought into play. Occasionally this yearning for uniqueness produces magazines that change format from time to time, even in successive issues. One such is the extraordinary *Lithopinion.* Another that has been off the beaten track for some years is *Aspen,* reaching the consumer either as loose contents in a box or as sheets in a portfolio or some other departure from bound pages.

The value of this diversity of appearance and formula was indicated in the 1960's and early 1970's when certain magazines were revived: the *Post* of the 1940's and the *Liberty* of 1925 to 1950. Then there were the several anthologies for *Liberty, Vanity Fair,* the *American,* the pulps and the comics.

VARIETY OF VIEWPOINTS

Possibly the most dramatic evidence of the astonishing variety among magazines is the spread of political and social viewpoints, convincing proof, as well, of the democratic nature of American society.

From the great journalistic smorgasbord table of magazine journalism the reader can sample any point of view. Such tasting has been made especially easy since the full arrival of the underground press, beginning in the 1960's. Every "ism" has its publication. Some isms have been so beset by schisms that there is a bewildering variety of similar publications, often bad-tempered and almost hysterical in tone.

For the ethically motivated liberal there is the thoughtful *Humanist.* The Norman Thomas brand of socialist has *Dissent,* almost a scholarly journal in tone. The extreme right offers its followers *American Opinion,* organ of the John Birch Society. *Commentary* is the voice of Jewish intellectuals, mostly in the liberal wing. The extreme left is represented by several periodicals echoing different Marxist angles: *New World Review* presents that outlook on the political and social scene. In this area, of course, are those war horses (although nowadays they would prefer to be called peace horses), the old and relatively widely-known *The Nation, The New Republic, The Progressive, Liberation* and *Commonweal,* on one side, and the *National Review* and *The Freeman,* on the other.

Courtesy of *Change* Magazine.
Cartoon by Rick Schreiter.

All the various shades of opinion in between have printed spokesmen, although they are not always in magazine format. They burgeon, not with advertising certainly, but with ideas for social reform that touch all areas of life. Then the reader has the choice of various pieces of important magazine journalism, coming largely from Europe and Canada.

Most U.S. magazines of opinion, such as the majority of those named above, are not easily available yet; a single newsstand cannot hold more than a fraction of them. But they are far more readily bought than they once were. Newsstand operators and magazine distributors used to refuse to handle them because of lack of demand and their reluctance to be associated with what they considered "extremist" publications, although certain of them that might be called rightist found places even though the demand was just as small for them as for the leftist. Most consumer magazines, until recent years, echoed conservative political and social views, as for instance the opinions of George Horace Lorimer, while editor of *The Saturday Evening Post,* and of Henry R. Luce, boss of Time Inc. Nowadays batches of "opinion" publications are delivered to the larger sales places, or are to be found in bookshops that make something of a specialty of them and the regular books to which they are akin. Greater public interest and activity in social problems in reflected in the opinion journals. Magazine sellers, therefore, have decided that money is to be made in putting such periodicals on display.

American magazines, as a whole, also are refreshing in all this diversity recounted here. The reader always is looking for surprises and often gets them. He may be overwhelmed when he sees their variety, but rewarded when he also sees his most detailed interests gratified within the pages of one of the 20,000. Perhaps he does not realize that magazines exist in a configuration: in circles.

4

The Circles of Magazines

APPARENTLY A WRITER ON a speciality subject amounts to something only if he designs a concept that is all his own. Marshall McLuhan stirred thinking when he advanced his hot and cool theory, for example. Therefore this book, not to be outdone in such matters, at this point notes a much less startling theory yet one that may be useful:

The magazines of any nation exist in circles corresponding to the circles created by the interests of the population.

At this time in American history those circles are changing their relationships. Until recently the larger ones hung in the journalistic universe like the great planets, with dozens of smaller ones, like stars, weaving in and out of the firmament around them. During the latter part of the 19th and the first half of the 20th centuries, the planets moved steadily in the heavens, challenged only by each other. The stars seemed to be mere satellites and of little influence. The dominant circles, at different times, bore such names as *The Saturday Evening Post, McCall's, Confidential, Collier's, McClure's* or *The Ladies' Home Journal,* to mention just a few. After a time some faded but new ones joined the survivors—the best known then being *Life, Look, Reader's Digest, Woman's Day* and several dozen more. These were enormous heavenly bodies of magazine journalism because they had comparatively huge circulations and, evidently, popular influence. It was not necessarily intensive influence; their lights shone brightly but did not penetrate the darkness. Being dependent upon the public they could not move much ahead of public opinion or lag too far behind. For, as is widely known in publishing, to do either soon leads to suicide. Cited can be instances of the *Literary Digest* and the first phase of *The Saturday*

Evening Post. The management of the first did not realize that America was changing in the 1920's and 1930's; the owners of the second ignored the shift until it was too late to battle television as well as internal management problems.

In the first half of this century the stars or smaller circles were periodicals of various social classes, but mainly the economic and educational upper middle and the center middle. There was *The New Yorker* circle, for instance, of the days of Harold Ross—the theater and literary sets congregated in New York City. After a while the magazine had more circulation outside the "Algonquin set" and the city itself than within them, and its circle expanded. Its formula, always a clue to the formation of a circle, was incapable of successful imitation. Publications in New York and various other cities tried it. *The Chicagoan, Chicago* and others of less obvious names appeared in that Illinois metropolis, for instance. Ross's magazine outlasted all, including *Park East,* which made a strong effort in New York.

But the best writers wanted to work for Ross, not because he paid particularly well (for he did not), but because of his literary standards and his coterie of writers and artists. They helped keep the ring healthy and firm. Today there is a new challenger with a somewhat similar name, *New York,* which has hung on for several years and is reported to be doing well. But it has its own editorial formula, as a comparison of the two will reveal and is competitive as well on the advertising level. *New York,* in short, is building its own circle, accumulating it as it spins.

The strength of a ring created by a magazine comes not only from an efficient business office and capable editors but also, and perhaps chiefly, from contributors. *The New Yorker* became strong because it had E. B. White and Katherine White, Wolcott Gibbs, Dorothy Parker, Ogden Nash, Helen Hokinson, Robert Benchley and more just as noted. Today its names are more international in their fame: Isaac Bashevis Singer, Arturo Vivante, Jean Stafford, John Updike and M. F. K. Fisher, for instance, mixed in with Richard Rovere, Winthrop Sargeant and some holdovers from the early times, like Gênet (Janet Flanner).

New York's ring, also, is dependent upon contributors with drawing power, such as Tom Wolfe and the liberationist, Gloria Steinem, who have their virtues but are of a different literary calibre from either Ross's group or those of William Shawn, the present *New Yorker* editor. *The New Yorker* circle was that of the sophisticated magazine, as it still is, but not a decadent sophistication. In that circle the others included *Vanity Fair,* now lost and invisible in the pages of dress pictures of *Vogue,* with which it was merged, and *Town and Country,* now much less than then for the horsey set. It was the sophistication of clever journalism: satire, more or less plotless fiction, observant biographies and insightful personality sketches, thoughtful editorializing, witty verse, and penetrating criticism of the arts, fine and popular.

Frank Mott once constructed a chart for the Macfadden publishing firm that graphically recorded the notable magazines, from the first in 1741 to recent times. The chart used bars; it could just as well have used circles to show the affinities. There was, as there is still, the band of scientific books, dominated by the astonishing *Scientific American,* which has been important if not always affluent since 1845 and never has cheapened or over-popularized science. With it have been the strictly technical magazines, like the *American Journal of Human Genetics,* popular treatments such as *Science and Mechanics* and hundreds of specialized journals, *The Laser Weekly* being among the recent additions.

Even the periodicals called radical, some of which today would be much more politically and socially acceptable than when they were published, existed as a group many years back. A number of the most famous were published in the 1920's and 1930's. Some still are going, surprisingly, but maybe not so surprisingly since these often are subsidized. The better known were called *Common Sense, New World Review, Marxist Review, The Catholic Worker, Communist International* and *The New Masses.* These were among the at least 65 available during those two decades. It was a small band of devoted readers that supported numerous magazines of tiny circulations and virtually no advertising. This circle has enlarged over the years since then because of new social conditions and a new awareness of society's problems among readers generally. Most of those who joined after 1930 did not last more than a few issues. *The Catholic Worker,* with a low-cost tabloid newspaper format but magazine content, has kept going, as has *New World Review. The Monthly Review* and the *International Socialist Review* also still are available. But the true radical press now is the underground, which is going around in a circle within the larger one.

And so there were, as there still are, circles of magazines for men, women and children as such—for farmers and fur merchants, gardeners and government workers, sport fans and smokers and many others with special interests.

Overlapping Circles

Readers may have been aware of such groupings perhaps without thinking of the magazines and of themselves as fitting into a geometrical pattern. In fact, readers may come within more than one circle. A journalist friend of the author owns a midwest berry farm. He also publishes magazines on special subjects, such as camping. For his business he keeps up with the subject of every magazine. For his private interests he reads specialized agricultural books. Several young writers known to the author subscribe to magazines on the dance. None of them can dance a ballet step, at least not gracefully. They read as spectators, as hobbyists and in one instance as a working critic, but not as performers. As performers they read periodicals on education, for one is a teacher; another reads the larger magazines for mothers and housekeepers, for she is both.

The author of this book is an even clearer case of varied interests met by magazine subscriptions; to the ones received and paid in advance must be added those seen in libraries or in exchanges of publications with friends. As a university teacher he saw the *Bulletin* of the American Association of University Professors. As a traveler he gets *Travel* and *Travel and Leisure*. As a frequent visitor to Scandinavia he receives *Norsk Ukeblad, Sweden Now* and *Look at Finland*. As a teacher of journalism and writer on that subject he regularly finds in his mailbox nine magazines concerned with the communications media. As a citizen the author turns to *Newsweek, World, Jet, The Nation, Saturday Review, Christian Century, Harper's, Commonweal* and *The New Republic* as a regular subscriber. *National Review, Atlantic, The Public Interest, New York Review of Books, Life, National Geographic* and *Time* are seen via newsstand purchase, the libraries or friends. All his other interests also are in magazine circles and these rings often intersect. So many magazines are in racks and stacks around the author's home that subscription salesmen who visit it are discouraged and stay instead to be interviewed about their selling methods. They cannot understand a person who has 65 subscriptions and reads another 40 magazines.

JOURNALISTIC AND ECONOMIC SIGNIFICANCE

The significance of these magazine circles is journalistic and economic. They do not exist economically in a totalitarian society like that of the Union of Soviet Socialist Republics, for there magazines go forth whether demanded or not. They are issued because government sees a specific purpose for them—to serve as promotion for particular ideas of social organization or as binding tissue for the social group. If a relatively few specialists need a magazine, they get it although its viewpoint may be warped, to be sure.

But the journalistic import of the circles exists in any society that is at all responsive to magazines. Thus in the Soviet Union, which is prolific in its production of technical journals, certain types of engineers or scientists have their periodicals. The circles of artists, writers and musicians similarly are supplied. Most widely known to the outside world, perhaps, are the literary journals, *Novy Mir* and *Zvezda*—which are heard about largely because of their involvement in disputes over certain authors holding unpopular views, such as Solzhenitzen, Ehrenberg and Yevtushenko.

One circle of magazines in the U.S.S.R., at least in form and function, is feeble in the U.S. magazine world: the satirical and humor periodical.

Although this country has a few (largely in the realm of the underground press) the Soviet Union is reported to have at least 20 of substance, led by *Krokodil.* The late James W. Markham, an American scholar of Russian and Chinese journalism, described this as intended to function like *The New Yorker* or *Punch,* although it "differs rather widely" from them and, he added, is "not always light in touch." Nevertheless, *Krokodil* reaches nearly three million people, which presumably is the number of readers, not subscribers.

The economic meaning of circles indeed is important in American publishing. For without a group of readers willing and able to support one or more, only isolated publications would exist, if any at all would go on without government subsidy. In the early years an American magazine usually was the sole journalistic output of a publisher—one firm, one magazine. It was all the owner could do to produce that. But when the book publishing companies entered the magazine business in the 19th century the idea of moving into other circles spread and has become common today. Harper & Brothers, still a leading book publishing firm but now called Harper & Row, at one time had magazines for four different readers' circles. *Harper's Monthly* was its general magazine; now it is a public affairs and quasi-literary periodical which dropped the *Monthly* long ago. A children's publication was called *Harper's Young People;* it lasted about two decades. *Harper's Bazaar,* the fashion magazine issued today by the Hearst Magazines organization, originally was a much less glamourous possession of the brothers. *Harper's Illustrated Weekly* was a news publication competing with the more famous *Frank Leslie's Illustrated.* Both were known for their woodcuts and are long gone.

Leslie, an English engraver whose real name was Henry Carter, in fact moved a dozen or more magazines into various circles. None of his output survives, although he and his later oft-married wife were extremely successful in their time. Out of such circling developed the large firms of multi-magazine publishers of this century: Curtis, Crowell-Collier and a dozen more as well equal that number in specialized circles, such as McGraw-Hill and Macfadden-Bartell. At its peak McGraw-Hill has had as many as 50 magazines at one time for various large and small circles of engineers, businessmen, managers and other specialists.

The Youth Magazines

When it comes to creating new specialty circles, one of the most successful publishing houses has been a firm of educational magazines whose output, or at least several of its magazines, is known in millions of American homes. Scholastic Magazines has not only a dozen periodicals but also publishes a library of supplemental readers and popular books for young people. Millions of school kids have reached, over the years, for *Junior* or *Senior Scholastic, World Week, Co-ed* or *Young Miss* among others, some of which had outlasted their usefulness in the early 1970's and were discontinued. Their teachers also have been provided with suitable periodicals. This output is part of a large circle identified as the juvenile magazines, also populated by such newsstand fare as *Seventeen, 16, Teen Screen, Teens* and *Ingenue.* Also trying to enter the life of the American teenager are the weekly story papers, as they are called, issued by various religious denomi-

"WHY AREN'T WE EXPOSING OBSCENITY LIKE ALL THE OTHER MAGAZINES?"

Copyright © 1969 The Chicago *Sun-Times* and reproduced by courtesy of Wil-Jo Associates and Bill Mauldin.

nations. If all children's and young people's journalism is considered a circle, the scope is even wider, for that admits not only such old timers as *Child Life* and *Jack and Jill* but also half a hundred church and newsstand periodicals aimed at youth. The latter include dozens of comic books and the varieties represented by *Hot Rod* and *Mad*.

The Sex-Oriented Magazines

An aged ring which has grown dramatically in the 1960's and 1970's is that of the magazine about sex or relying on sex appeal. Like some other groups, actually it is a circle with smaller ones within it, somewhat like a cone. At the narrow end are the magazines of hard-core pornography, largely imported and far more underground than the so-called underground press. Because of postal regulations this scabrous printed matter is harder to find or to obtain than the porno film, which has become visible in many cities at downtown theaters. But there they are in a tight little enclosure of their own.

Around them, occupying a somewhat larger ring, are the magazines that explore sex in word and picture. Among the unsubtle titles is one called *Screw*. Their content, unlike that of the porno books, is broader than sex for it is a mixture of that, politics, material on the ecology, organic gardening and orthodox humor among other subjects and forms.

Occupying the next circle, but still small, are the supposedly serious, scientifically directed magazines with such respectable titles as *Sexology* and *Sexual Behavior,* the former founded as long ago as 1923, the second issued first in 1971. They are disappointing to the merely curious, for some articles are almost unintelligible to readers who depend upon cartoons and photographs for their communication.

In the next larger band are magazines for people who want a generous offering of sex-emphasis material that is not clinically so specific as to be boring. These are symbolized by *Playboy* for the men and *Cosmopolitan* for the women. Some others pretend that they contain what such readers seek. *Girl Talk,* to be seen only at milady's beauty parlor, is one such. Says an advertisement caption: *"Girl Talk* is sexier than that Cosmopolitan Girl." The copy mentions the queen of this circle, *Cosmo,* which has ten times *Girl Talk*'s circulation but the same essential appeal—to those young women eager for help in trapping men into marriage or some other sort of relationship. These periodicals are not alone, but their imitators usually are quickies that exist for an issue or two and then drop away.

Playboy, on the other hand, heads a parade of fairly stable magazines that have been in the circle with it for some time: *Cavalier, Rogue, Stag* and others with their nudie foldouts, cartoons and jokes *à la* the leader. The closest competitor is *Penthouse,* a recent invader from Britain. But none has *Playboy*'s serious articles on public problems, the work of leading novelists and the contributions of deep-thinking professional philosophers. And none of these printed substitutes for sexual realities has gone into a Braille edition, as has *Playboy,* in a cruel joke on the blind, for they are sent the text only.

THE FAN MAGAZINES

Possibly one of the most astonishing of circles is that of the fan magazines to be found in the realms of sports, movies, broadcasting, the theater and other aspects of the entertainment and leisure-time world. Irving Shulman, the novelist and screen playwright, has disclosed much about a group of these magazines in a book, *"Jackie,"* tracing their treatment of Mrs. Jacqueline Kennedy Onassis. Of interest here are his discoveries about their readers, given in more detail in his book. Some highlights only: They are read almost 100 per cent by women. A survey team found only 35 men out of 1,917 persons who went to the supermarket racks to buy these publications. When the men were asked "Why?" 32 answered in some fashion that boiled down to "My neighbor's wife reads this 'crap' and asked me to get it for her. Frankly, he'd rather have her read this than run around, drink or smoke pot." Of the 1,882 women, half were in the 26–45 age range. Only 164 were under 20, and 135 over 50. About 375 were between 21 and 25; 265 between 46 and 50.

And why did the women buy them? Almost 1,100 said they bought them for neighbors, relatives or friends; about 800 said for themselves. When asked the reason for buying them for themselves the main single answer was "to get interesting low-down on people." The second important reason was that these magazines give their readers something to talk about. Unable to discuss public affairs, the readers welcomed the stars' personal problems as revealed in *Screen Stars, Movie Life, Photoplay, TV-Radio Mirror* and the like.

THE CIRCLES' INFLUENCE

Circles of magazine readers, as we have seen, depend upon advertising appeal. Perhaps it would be more nearly accurate to say that advertisers exploit the circles. It is illustrated in a humorous way by a Weber cartoon in *The New Yorker* in which a discouraged electric shaver salesman standing near a large counter card says to an indifferent departing potential customer. "But it's advertised in '*Life.*' Doesn't that mean anything to you?"

Whether any one of these circles is vicious, the readers of this book must determine for themselves. Readers can at least play the game of

Cartoon by Edmund C. Arnold.

determining which circles they travel in, which they help to keep alive and moving. Most of us probably do not think of our magazine consumption in that particular way, although in this day of growing consumer consciousness perhaps it is easier to achieve such an awareness than ever before. Obviously the regular buyer of *Cosmopolitan* or *Bachelor* has little self-consciousness about identifying with his or her magazine. To observe how readers often dress *à la* the advertising in one or the other of their favorite magazines indicates no reluctance to be classified as a *Cosmo* girl or a *Playboy* playboy. On the contrary.

Russell Baker, the New York *Times'* humorous essayist, once used his "The Observer" column to have fun in guessing at what people were like, judging by the magazines on their coffee tables. He reported an alleged conversation between a *Playboy* Reader, a *Cosmopolitan* Girl and a *New Republic* Subscriber. The N.R. Subscriber complains because Miss Girl is listening to Stravinsky music on records and disturbing guests in his downstairs apartment. P. Reader comes in, talks only about his clothes and

Miss Girl vainly hints to both about her lack of a date for that evening. But the two men soon depart. *Cosmo* Girl, in tears, begins eating a copy of her favorite periodical, consumes it all and ends with a famous line from its advertising: ". . . at least my magazine understands me."

As readers we are all within magazine circles. But we do not, as the *Cosmo* Girl is made to say, always find out that our magazines understand us. In fact, many that failed to understand us have disappeared. Were the readers in their circles the only force that had that effect?

5

The Affected Magazines

THE EXISTENCE OF various types of readers, of a wide variety of periodicals and of innumerable circles of magazines creates publication problems. It takes an alert and skilled management indeed, these days, to launch and keep alive a new periodical, particularly in the unsubsidized business world of journalism. The American tradition of a legally unfettered press makes it possible for anyone to start a new magazine at any time. Obstacles there are, to be sure, but they are not of the type imposed in totalitarian countries, such as government ownership or control of all publications and fines or imprisonment if content is critical of the regime.

That very freedom means, however, a rise in competition, a right that has endowed the nation with a magazine press of many views, as noted. The forces of change therefore can affect magazines in such a way as to destroy them. They become vulnerable to the economic and social pressures that characterize a *laissez faire* society.

Possibly the worst effect on the magazines is the idea held by readers that because a few giants have been killed by a combination of the forces for change the publishing industry as a whole is in trouble. And because some of these readers also are advertisers or potential advertisers, the resulting lack of confidence can be fatal. In this respect magazines are like banks. A rumor about one can result in a run that could destroy it and others with it. Tales of magazines on the skids float around Madison Avenue constantly; most are untrue, spread by gossip columnists and careless news media as well as wishful thinkers. Advertisers are like depositors or racing enthusiasts. They naturally do not wish to spend money on a publication lacking public confidence. Who bets knowingly on a likely loser?

44

DEATHS AND BIRTHS

The list of magazine casualties in the 1960's and early 1970's includes hundreds of titles. The great majority were highly specialized and, for various reasons, ill-fated from birth. During the period more new magazines were issued (and have survived) than those that failed—a net numerical gain. The Magazine Publishers Association, which tries to keep records on the industry, compiled a table showing the number of periodicals sold, merged or discontinued, and new ones introduced between 1962 and 1971. It found that 160 had ceased publication and that 753 were begun. The reading public, however, usually hears only of the big-name periodicals and seldom knows about the specialized journals. Thus, beginning in the late 1950's, readers heard of the failure of *Colliers', Woman's Home Companion* and the *American.* Then came the end of *Coronet,* the merging of *Show Business Illustrated* (a *Playboy* venture) with *Show* and then the disappearance, off and on, of *Show* itself. The big shock came in 1969 when *The Saturday Evening Post* was halted. Then, in 1971 and 1972, *Look* and *Life* were killed, causing equally great tremors in the industry. There were others, such as *American Weekly* and *This Week,* from that outland known as the magazine supplement to newspapers. Like most of the rest, however, they too were multi-million circulation publications. (See App. 3.)

Coronet, Show, the *Post* and even the old *Liberty* were reborn under new owners, with a similar editorial formula for the latter two: emphasis on nostalgia. But to the older reader the departure of these magazines came against a background of other notable losses that occurred during the first six decades of this century: *Literary Digest, Vanity Fair,* the *Delineator, Better Living, Everywoman's* and *American Boy,* for instance.

It made no difference that in the second and third quarters of the century numerous new magazines were born and still flourish. It is an impressive roll call: *The New Yorker, TV Guide, The Reader's Digest, Yachting, Sports Illustrated, Ebony, Seventeen, Mademoiselle, Jet, Glamour, Psychology Today, Saturday Review, Esquire, Playboy, Time, True, Mad, Newsweek, U.S. News & World Report, Ingenue, Fortune, Woman's Day, Family Circle.*

The stories behind three of the most widely publicized failures of recent years perhaps will reveal the complexity of the economic stresses and influences on magazines. These accounts may help to answer the oft-put question: But why do they fail?

THE *Coronet* STORY

The uncrowning of *Coronet* illustrates the difficulties that beset a publication that is ahead of its time. Arnold Gingrich, its actual first editor (and also of *Esquire,* of which he was still the publisher in 1973) has told the story of the monthly's early days in his memoirs issued in 1971. Its life also portrays what happens to a magazine aimed at a public too small to maintain it or to one which insists on appealing to a mass readership with material intended for a limited circle of readers.

Because a somewhat similar magazine of the same name still is on the newsstands, many readers are aware of *Coronet.* But to use the word *similar* confuses the situation. During its life under its original, and the present, owners of a *Coronet* that continued one of the formulas for a time, the magazine has had five distinct personalities as its editors sought for the most satisfactory one.

Esquire was so successful in 1936 that David Smart, owner of the firm bearing his name and later called Esquire, Inc., decided on a venture of his own. He and William H. Weintraub were co-publishers of *Esquire,* but Smart had a pet idea he wanted to try out: a pocket-size magazine, without advertising, to be sub-titled "Infinite Riches in a Little Room." Intended, as Gingrich put it, "to give the public what it ought to like, whether it liked it or not," it was called *Coronet.* If it made no money Smart was not concerned, for the losses would be useful in tax calculations.

The magazine's first personality was artistic, somewhat like that of *Horizon* today. Its early issues beginning in 1936 were decorated with pictures of Persian miniatures and were a place for clever and artistic writing. It was pocket-size, hence the "little room." It sold amazingly well at first, despite its esoteric content. Then it began to decline. A new editor made no changes, so the decline was not stemmed. Oscar Dystel, taking over in 1940, turned *Coronet* around completely. It became an imitation of *Reader's Digest,* divested of its exclusiveness, originality and artistic appeal. Inspiration now was the theme, not Christopher Marlowe's "Infinite Riches." And it worked. Sales rose.

By using the printing paper for *Esquire* in a certain way, Smart saved *Coronet* during World War II, when stock shortages and government control hurt other magazines. Circulation mounted as much as ten-fold in the boom years during and just after the war. Theodore Peterson, historian of this century's magazines, reports that some estimates reach five million. That it hit two million at least is indicated by the guarantee of that circulation to advertisers, after the decision to sell space had been reached.

A third personality was being expressed after advertising entered the pages. Now there was less inspirational material, more varied reader participation content appeared, such as puzzles and games, as did somewhat more serious articles. New editors included Harris Shevelson and Lewis Gillenson. The latter was to be its last under Esquire, Inc., ownership. For in 1961, the magazine's press was sold to *Reader's Digest* and its subscription list split between the latter and Curtis Publishing Co. By the late 1950's losses again were being suffered. These, Peterson learned, amounted to about $600,000 a year. Circulation when death came stood at nearly three million. *Coronet* had lasted exactly a quarter of a century, its final issue being dated October, 1963. Gingrich said in a speech two years later that there had been "insufficient riches in too little room," i.e., not enough advertising revenue.

Still one more personality was imparted to *Coronet* when another firm, H.S. Publications, brought out a physically similar *Coronet* in the same year. A suit brought by the Reader's Digest Association to prevent use of the name and further publication was lost. The revival went in for general interest materials, such as topical articles on family problems, man-woman relationships and self-help guidance pieces. It competed more with the old rival, *Pageant,* than with the *Digest.* This formula persisted until 1972, when the fifth personality was introduced by another new owner, Warner Communications—NPP Communications Group Division. *Coronet* became a women's psychological service periodical.

The extent of the face- and content-lifting given *Coronet* in 1972 is illustrated by the virtual reversal of its formula. Inspired by the success of *Cosmopolitan,* the greater timeliness of some new women's magazines, and a supposed change in the attitude of women toward their life styles of domesticity or being second-class citizens in the business world, *Coronet* went in for more current events and behind-the-scenes articles. At the same time, according to its advertising manager, it avoided muckraking and sex-book content (he appeared to equate them). The editor directing the implementation of the editorial change, Mrs. Yvonne Dunleavy, co-authored a book called *The Happy Hooker.*

How was it possible for a magazine with several millions in circulation to fail, the reader repeats? It is a question that usually overlooks a simple fact: consumer magazines are business enterprises. Their activities are conceived by many owners as being no more artistic or romantic than the canning of food or the operation of transportation firms. Such a question derives from the long-held belief that, given plenty of circulation—sale of newsstand and subscription copies—a magazine must thrive, for is not the advertising dependent upon such distribution? In less competitive days, in days when it cost less to produce magazines, that view was correct. But with the burgeoning of television and increases in the cost of manufacture of the copies, advertisers had an alternative means of reaching a national mass audience that they deemed more effective and therefore less expensive.

That they can do that more cheaply, efficiently, profitably and effectively via the home screen still is debated and cannot be settled here. If agencies and advertisers think so, to that extent magazines will have a smaller share of the advertising dollar than they might have otherwise. In the late 1950's and early 1960's publishers still were trying to achieve box-car circulation figures so as to combat television. Several expensively-produced magazines stood in the ranks of 8 million to 15 million circulation until the costs of printing and distributing such huge quantities became too burdensome and conservative publishers spoke out for restraint. *Coronet* had succumbed to the competitive pressure. The harm had been done before it could be saved.

As with any other commercial business, income must more than equal outgo. A magazine publishing firm normally has only two major sources of revenue: advertising and circulation. That was particularly so in the 1950's, when diversification was not so common as in the 1960's and 1970's. Obviously, if costs outstrip income, trouble occurs. This fate struck the Crowell-Collier publications which died a few years before *Coronet*. Death came to the three stalwarts when they were at the peak of their circulations. Although there was more advertising sold than ever before, it did not offset the steady rise of all costs: editorial, paper, printing, mailing and rents, principally. *More* simply was not *enough*.

Another factor: H.S. Publications, for a time *Coronet's* owner in the early years of its revival, like Esquire, Inc., was a multiple publishing firm. Esquire had published not only *Esquire* and *Coronet* but also *Ken, Verve* and *Gentleman's Quarterly*. H.S. was issuing *Confidential* and *Blue Book* when it launched the new *Coronet*. Thus either firm may have been in a position to sustain a loss leader, as *Coronet* must have been considered by its owners. Esquire, Inc., did so for several years; H.S. (the initials of its then owner, Hy Stierman) guarded facts about the firm's operations so *Coronet's* balance sheet is not available.

By 1972 the magazine had been owned by several more new firms. By that year it had an audited circulation, on a monthly average, of 350,000. Most sales were single copy, only about 13,500 persons getting it by mail. With low subscription figures some overhead could be saved. But the magazine may have been carried by the NPP Paperback Library, a large book business and another operation of the Warner Publishing Co.

Frequent changes in personality, depending upon the temperaments of the readers, can harm or help a magazine. A reader who dislikes change so much that he resists it in all aspects of life naturally is impatient with a magazine that no longer conveys his own image of it.

One reason that *Reader's Digest* has been so successful is that it has changed little since it was founded in 1922. Its price has more than doubled but so has the amount of material offered readers. Originally it carried no advertising, but since 1955 has done so. The over-all small, convenient size is the same. All articles at first were reprinted from other publications but today much copy is bought and placed in the others by the *Digest* itself, yet readers seem not to consider that an important policy change. Essentially the magazine is the same, for in point of view it hardly has varied, being consistently conservative both socially and politically. Its many short pieces and departments please busy Americans as well as the middle classes of 169 other countries or areas where it is sold. The *Digest* has been able to survive handsomely despite its conservatism whereas *The Saturday Evening Post,* holding to much the same social philosophy failed. The *Digest* has been able to cope because its management has been wiser in other respects: what changes have been made occurred gradually, not abrasively; it has remained handily portable in size; it has maintained a strong reader-participation policy with its content; it has stressed personal problems of readers, offering what is considered advice on some of the most intimate difficulties people experience.

Shops in big cities often carry back issues of magazines. The yellow covers of *National Geographic* are ranged for many years into the past on the shelves and look much alike. The photography has improved as has the color reproduction but the basic formula is unaltered. That is the way its readers want it.

On the other hand, readers of magazines much different from the *Digest* and the *Geographic,* such as *Ramparts, National Lampoon* and *The New York Review of Books,* like changes in the personality of their publications. Perhaps this is so because their social stance is likely to conform to that of each magazine, since they are persons who appear to favor the experimental in many aspects of living. Such publications can therefore make innumerable changes in content and presentation with little, if any, protest so long as the ideology is not altered.

Thus *Coronet's* five personalities harmed it in the long run. Because the first was ahead of its day, it was not viable. The second alienated the original reader, but won many more readers of another type. Yet the magazine never was the actual front-runner in its class, for it always was second to the *Digest.* Eventually it went down to 10 per cent of its best circulation figure. Devoid of important influence at all times, *Coronet* was pure entertainment and so has been just "another magazine" after its first years of aesthetic distinction. Its editors' newest formula may tell a different story, for they are currently seeking to give it a niche of its own.

THE *Saturday Evening Post* STORY

The natural function of the American economy explains the birth, death and rebirth of *Coronet.* But a similar life story for the *Post* requires a different explanation—a far more elaborate situation is interwoven with the fate of the Curtis Publishing Co., which already has been the subject of five books, one of them a novel, and innumerable articles.

No collapse of a modern magazine empire has equalled that of Curtis, owner of *The Saturday Evening Post* and other large magazines, unless it was that of Crowell-Collier which had about the same number of units when it dispatched them in 1956 and 1957. The operations of each of these large corporations were complex and undoubtedly confusing to the layman. Each firm was deeply affected by strong changes occurring in the world of mass communications. And each was the victim of administrative indecision, mistakes in judgment and corporate infighting. Perhaps the Curtis troubles seem the more severe just because its flagship periodical, the *Post,* had been in the public eye for so many years.

To understand the effects of the various forces working on the *Post* it is necessary to review briefly the events leading up to its decline and fall, as one *Post* staff member, Otto Friedrich, dubbed it.

That the magazine had a bucolic tone during most of its life was not surprising. Its long-time owner, Cyrus H. K. Curtis, founder of the Curtis Publishing Co., began his career by bringing out *The Tribune and Farmer,* a 4-page weekly, in 1879. When his wife, Louisa Knapp Curtis, hooted at the "Women and Home" department and—after having been given responsibility for it—improved it, he made the page a monthly supplement and then, in 1883, expanded it into *The Ladies' Home Journal.* Twelve years later he added another magazine . . . what was then the nearly dead *Post.*

Originally founded in 1821 and not, as the magazine's later publishers asserted, in 1728 by Benjamin Franklin, *The Saturday Evening Post* was a popular weekly issued in Philadelphia. After the Civil War it went into a slow decline and by 1895 was faltering badly and seemed near extinction. The editor was a moonlighting local reporter who was paid $10 a week to clip exchanges and do the minimum otherwise. When Curtis was appealed to, he bought it for $1,000.

In time the *Post* was put on its feet by its first great editor, George Horace Lorimer, who converted it into an important force in American journalism as the socially and politically conservative voice of the group now considered "middle America." It also became an attractive goal for many of the country's best writers of popular fiction. But by the early 1940's the magazine was beginning to face new and strong competition, notably from broadcasting and from other magazines, particularly *Life, Look* and *Time.* The Curtis people were unwilling, at the same time, to venture into a policy of diversification now so common among large publishing houses. So the seeds of trouble were being sown in those years. Ben Hibbs came on as editor. The magazine was changed typographically, non-fiction stressed, more photographs scheduled and other policies followed to produce a new *Post*. In a few years the activities of the whole firm had broadened; by the end of World War II Curtis also was publishing *The Ladies' Home Journal, Jack and Jill* and *Country Gentleman. Holiday* soon was added. Curtis at that time also owned a large printing plant, a subsidiary company, certain lands and other buildings and further related holdings.

The *Post,* along with the other Curtis enterprises, went along smoothly until the arrival of television competition. The new medium was to shake up the magazine industry in the 1950's by distracting readers and channeling to itself much of the money of advertisers who heretofore had relied primarily on newspapers and magazines to reach the mass public. The Curtis management, reported James Playsted Wood, a Curtis insider for many years, was worried about the power of TV but "shook its communal head and repeated its standard declaration: 'We're in the publication business.' " More seeds of future trouble were dropping.

And by the end of the decade the trouble had grown. Crowell-Collier, rival publisher of three stalwarts of American magazinedom—*Collier's, Woman's Home Companion* and the *American*—had killed them, although Curtis was not yet seriously feeling the effects. Another face-lifting had taken place at the *Post* but, by 1959, more drastic means were needed not only for it but for other Curtis magazines of which one, *Country Gentleman,* had already been cut off after a long life. New editorial personnel came in, with ideas for the *Post's* content and presentation. Nevertheless, in 1961 the company showed a huge deficit.

An account of the changes in management and staff during the next eight years is so complex that a writer of the company's history, Otto Friedrich, drew a chart for the end papers of his book on the magazine's decline and fall to help make the story clear. The main point, for the purpose here, is to note that the firm fell into the hands of boards of directors that sought to change policy but whose methods were not always suitable for effective magazine publishing management. Revolt within the ranks created what amounted to civil war.

By not keeping up with the social changes that were occurring in the nation, the *Post* was hurt. When it did recognize the necessity, it was too late. Financial losses continued, assets were wiped out, employes dismissed by the hundreds. Huge libel suits added to the problem, some the result of hasty editorial work. Regular contributors were mistreated, as were staff personnel. Internal disputes were common. As have other businesses in financial trouble, Curtis caught the interest of a lawyer-banker and dealer in sick companies named Martin S. Ackerman. In 1968 he gave Curtis a $5-million loan and was named president. He added a classic quotation to the lore of magazine history when he introduced himself to the Curtis officers and staff thus: "I am Marty Ackerman. I am 36 years old and I am very rich."

Ackerman promised prosperity for the firm, saying he did not intend to sell any Curtis publications and that under his presidency the *Post* would continue. He began his therapy by disposing of the Philadelphia building, long a famous tourist attraction on Independence Square. Next went a paper mill. Hundreds more were taken off the payroll. He cut the *Post's* circulation from 7 million to 3½ million, arousing ire among some long-time subscribers. The emphasis was to be on choice, class-magazine appeal —catering to the financially better-heeled. An amusing sidelight was provided by the eccentricities of computerism. Among those none-too-well-off subscribers chopped from the list were Winthrop Rockefeller, then governor of Arkansas, and Ackerman himself. Four months after having taken over, Ackerman sold *The Ladies' Home Journal* and *American Home* to Downe Publishing Co. The *Post, Holiday, Jack and Jill* and a newcomer, *Status,* struggled on in a maze of economic deals. Wood reports that the firm had a $20 million deficit in 1968.

Then, in early February 1969, the *Post* itself was killed.

Within a few months the firm was in chaos. Ackerman resigned as president and as board chairman. He had served without salary. Its big printing plant closed, leaving hundreds more workers jobless; other properties were sold. After much litigation Curtis regained three magazines, which for a time had gone to an Ackerman-owned firm; these were *Holiday, Jack and Jill* and *Status.* It also obtained full rights to the *Post.* But the *Journal* and *American Home* were elsewhere. Shortly *Status,* which never had amounted to much with its purely snob-appeal content, was sold to *Show.*

Beurt Ser Vaas became Curtis' new owner in 1970. Described by Lacey Fosburgh of the New York *Times* as "a self-made millionaire who has developed numerous successful businesses through the Middle West," Ser Vaas revived the *Post* as a quarterly to be directed toward the "middle American." Its $1-a-copy issues have been reproductions of the old *Post,* including content, and contained no exposés or muckraking. As for the company itself, Ser Vaas sold all its manufacturing units, cut the staffs down to about 100, paid off debts and proceeded to issue not only the *Post* but also its old companions, *Holiday* and *Jack and Jill,* more or less along their original formulas.

THE *Look* STORY

Despite the gloomy forecasts of the inside dopesters, few people in the industry really expected to see another leading mass magazine succumb to the forces for change. Readers, even though unaware of the details of big-time magazine publishing, were not so surprised. They had been prepared by the other recent failures. Also, it may be said that American journalistic news-philosophy inevitably leads people to assume the worst. The news media, printed or electronic, report the exceptional rather than the ordinary event. After a few such pieces of news, readers accept the exceptional as the norm. If a few muggings occur the streets henceforth are flooded with muggers. If a score of students break windows at six colleges, the campi of the several thousand other such institutions are in chaos. If several large magazines fail, the entire industry is collapsing.

The next giant to go—to the chopping block—was Cowles Communication's *Look.* Gardner Cowles, its founder, had said to Ann Ray Martin, a *Newsweek* writer: "My heart is in *Look*—it's my baby. I founded it 33 years ago. I'd sell everything to keep it going." That was in September, 1970. Thirteen months later the final issue came off the press, dated Oct. 19, 1971.

In the meantime Cowles had disposed of all the other magazines owned by Cowles Communications, Inc., as well as certain holdings other than periodicals. In fact, the efforts to retrench had begun well before fall of 1970, for *Look* had been in trouble since 1968. Magazine readers may recognize only a few of the properties disposed of. They included:

> *Education News,* an experiment with broad, quick coverage of its specialty. Discontinued.
> Suffolk (N.Y.) *Sun,* a Long Island newspaper, also new. Killed.
> San Juan (Puerto Rico) *Sun,* a daily. Sold.
> Ocala *Star-Banner,* Gainesville *Sun,* and Lakeland *Ledger,* all Florida papers. Sold.
> *Family Circle,* a multi-million circulation women's magazine sold mainly in supermarkets. Sold.
> Ten trade magazines, known collectively as the Magazines for Industry. Sold.
> WREC-TV, a Memphis, Tenn., station. Sold.
> A group of seven medical magazines. Sold.
> The Cambridge Book Co., a textbook firm. Sold.
> *Venture,* a magabook of jet-set travel and leisure living. Discontinued.

When Mike Cowles, as Gardner Cowles was more familiarly known, announced the death of *Look* on Aug. 16, 1971, he explained: "As we considered this action, my heart said, 'Keep it going,' but my head said, 'Suspend it,' and there really was no other way."

When stopped, *Look,* a bi-weekly most of its life, had 6½ million circulation. Its losses, Cowles said, as reported by the New York *Times,* were "well in excess of ten million dollars" during the preceding two-and-a-half years. Some of the properties sold (and not all are listed above) were profitable, others were a serious drain on the company.

As with the other dead giants of magazinedom, efforts were made to explain and understand the reasons for the demise. Some of them will sound familiar by now. Cowles himself listed the causes that promoted the board of directors' decision. They were, he said:

1. "The economy went sour." *Look* lost more and more as the economy degraded.
2. Network television hurt advertising revenues.
3. Costs rose steadily. Certain costs—and here he pointed to the postal rate increases—were not possible for management to control.

Other persons had additional explanations. *Newsweek's* writers noted certain misjudgments of management, such as the founding of the Long Island paper to begin with, for it is reported to have lost the firm a total of $15-million. Another attributed speeches made in 1970 by the magazine's publisher, Thomas R. Shephard, Jr., who had expressed an ultra-conservative social philosophy before advertising groups. *Look,* for most of its life, had been credited with a small measure of liberalism and tolerance of social change in the direction of what might be called progress. Thus Shephard created a contradiction that confused advertisers. 'Was *Look* liberal or not, they wondered.

Explanations of a still different kind came from publishing and advertising executives. John Mack Carter, president of Downe Publishing Co., told *Advertising Age,* for instance, that the loss of *Look* was unnecessary and could have been avoided. Its problems, he said, were not unique. But he added that the Cowles management "tended to postpone correction of its problems to a point where it seemed that dissolution . . . was the best course."

What Carter then observed was clearly critical of the Cowles administration. Until late in 1970, he noted, the magazine's financial troubles "could have been brought to manageable proportions." But he did not indicate how. He went on to say that Cowles had lost its dedication to publishing, thus creating an atmosphere in which it was impossible for any magazine to exist. Don Gussow, the successful publisher of a group of business magazines which he had sold to Cowles and then re-purchased, was a member of the Cowles board. In a 1972 book (*Divorce Corporate Style*) on the inner workings at Cowles, Gussow supports Carter's observations with convincing detail.

By the time *Life* died at the end of 1972 the general public and the industry alike had a feeling of *déjà vu*. But was it merely the rest of the play, *"Life's* Labor Lost"? Had we seen Act. I (*Collier's*), Act. II, (*The Saturday Evening Post*), Act. III (*Look*), Act. IV, (*Life*)? Or was there something different about the last act?

Most of the major causes of death of the 36-year-old weekly picture magazine corresponded to the reasons for the decease of the others:

1. Costs of production continued to rise.
2. Costs of distribution, already at their highest, were scheduled to rise steeply.
3. Advertising revenue, although improving, was not up to necessities.
4. Enormous losses were being absorbed by management.
5. Television was providing a larger mass audience.
6. Special interest magazines were growing rapidly in number and circulation.
7. Circulation drops made by management did not produce the expected results.
8. Advertising rates were high enough to cut out many small advertisers despite demographic editions.

Two other causes held true in the earlier deaths but did not in the instance of *Life:* 1. Mismanagement. 2. General company weakness.

1. After the event there was less of the accusation of mismanagement and bad judgment that had been directed particularly at the publishers of *Collier's,* the *Post,* and *Look.* Before the obituary was written, to be sure, some other magazine executives had ideas for saving *Life* (see *New York* for Oct. 23, 1972) but their changes were not of the sort that could overcome the imponderables of the situation (items 1, 2, 5, and 6 above).
2. *Life's* companion magazines—*Time, Fortune, Sports Illustrated* and even the brand new *Money*—were not in trouble. In the instances of the earlier dead giants, the trouble within the firm was widespread.

Scores of smaller magazines have duplicated the experiences of the *Post* and *Look* in miniature in recent years as well. Most had no diversification of operations to fall back upon to help them through crises, as Time Inc. had and was thus able to save *Life* until late 1972 with revenue from *Time, Fortune,* and *Sports Illustrated,* radio and newspaper operations. These little publications were individually-owned trade journals, or church-owned periodicals, or house magazines serving a single company's employees or customers. Living on subsidy is often the only way to keep some of these members of the journalism family in the publishing business. Those that died were victims largely of sky-rocketing costs of operation combined with falling revenues for their owners, particularly in the instance of company magazines. And revenue of the churches from their members fell off as the economy created greater joblessness and high living costs. The business periodical lost advertising and subscriptions in the face of increased expenses of its own.

THE *Cosmopolitan* STORY

How were some of the other giants affected? Why did the advertising volume and revenue of various magazines climb steadily at the same time that the three examples recounted here were declining in fiscal health?

Essentially the answer comes down to certain basic principles of magazine publishing. An unnamed magazine executive gave part of the answer to Joseph O'Keefe, a Washington *Star* staff writer, when he was describing the industry's troubles in the early 1970's. He said: "Unless you've got a well-defined editorial purpose and are well-managed you're dead."

Death has indeed changed certain magazines, as we have seen. But others that might have been the subjects of obituaries have gone on with new formulas. *Cosmopolitan,* an old-timer started in Rochester, N.Y., in 1886 but owned since 1905 in New York City by the Hearst magazines firm, now has that well-defined policy. It has had more phases even than *Coronet.* At first it was a *pot-pourri* of travel and biography, then as what a later editor called the "university of the mind," for a time an editorial genius named Ray Long combined easy cultural copy with popular fiction, emphasizing the narrative. Next came a more intellectual formula, but unsuccessfully, according to Peterson the historian. The general appeal dominated once again until it began to flag in the early 1960's.

When, in 1965, it received an injection from a new editor it was soon realized that the doctor had prescribed well. Men had been editing *Cosmopolitan* all through the years. This doctor was a woman: Helen Gurley Brown. Today she continues to be at least as well known for her books as her editing—*Sex and the Single Girl* probably is her best-known opus.

The change Mrs. Brown worked at *Cosmopolitan* is represented by the remark so often heard, that it has become "a *Playboy* for women." This image was sharpened in 1972 when *Cosmo* carried as a centerspread a picture of a male nude. The focus of the content is on what women can do to attract men and on encouraging less-than-beauteous young women to believe there really is no problem for them to do so. It was this concern that led to Mrs. Brown's appointment. Certainly it was not experience in magazine editing, for she had had none, although she had been in the advertising business—which is not so far afield as some might think.

The *Cosmopolitan* editorial policy, as has been stated in Standard Rate & Data Service Reports, is that it "is edited for young women, married and single, interested in self-improvement, careers, clothes, beauty, travel, entertainment and the arts . . . with special emphasis on the world outside the home. It is edited to help young women realize the very best of themselves."

This bland statement contrasts with the actual expression of the formula in content. For most of its life *Cosmo* has been conventional in viewpoint. But Mrs. Brown has changed that. It is not that she is a philosopher in depth, basing her editing on sociological studies of changes in American life style. She believes she knows her readers' basic interests. Like all competent commercial editors, she gives them what interests her and, since she is one with her readers, they accept the fare eagerly.

This fact was illustrated during the month when the magazine carried its pin-up of Burt Reynolds, a then minor actor willing to strip for the pose and delighted to be announced in the magazine as The Perfect Man. The total enjoyment of the gag picture among many women of between 20 to 40 years of age pleases the editor. The author, for example, saw an enthusiastic reader take her copy down the aisle of a train to show the picture of Apollo to several eager friends who had merely heard talk about it. She was careful to recover it from them and put it under lock and key in her suitcase before leaving the train. No college boy could have been more protective of his copy of *Playboy* than she was of that issue of *Cosmopolitan*.

But the female form also is part of the formula of success. Young girls in few clothes are numerous enough in its pages to attract men readers, husbands or male pals, perhaps. Certain of the article titles would draw in these extra readers: As for example, "The Nice Girls Who Appear in Pornographic Movies," with pictures of the girls at their sexiest if not at their barest.

The forces for change that affected *Cosmopolitan* were prophetic waves from the brain of Helen Gurley Brown. Long before, as had many other persons but few magazine editors, she had been aware of a changing attitude in the United States toward sexuality and a never-satisfied interest in people. Ever since the mid-1960's, such forces have kept this magazine successful. And those same forces have kept healthy, at least in an economic way, other magazines that have also been responsive. The changing attitude toward sex is a major factor in magazine publishing (as well as in book publishing and film-making) and needs to be better understood. It is evident in several ways, such as is demonstrated in publications' freedom in their discussions of sexual topics, in the free use of sex and medical terms, and in the candor—some people would call it tastelessness—of illustrations on the covers and inside magazines that are seen on newsstands or in homes.

What publications feel free to print reflects the social change that has been occurring. Youth, women's and ethnic minority movements have broken the barriers, both in language and personal relationships. Once not tolerated, topless women entertainers appear in most cities. Bikinis on the beach are standard wear and miniskirts have been common garb. Even prostitution has been changed by the new freedom, the professionals complaining of the "amateur" competition. Sex advice is provided now by daily newspapers as well as popular magazines; never has it been so graphic and candid. Literature once forbidden is in everyone's reach; pornography, whatever that may be, is sold in grimy stores in many communities. These observations are not made in moral judgment but merely to illustrate the point about a trend that affects magazines.

So the *Cosmopolitan* promotion department had something to work with under the Brown regime, such as "The Sexually Obsessed Woman," a typical title; on the cover, an observant reader noticed, it was "The Sexually Obsessed Girl," however. And in another, "Dr. Reuben Lets You in on the Secrets of Male Sexuality (To Help You Win That Man)." For some years now full-page advertisements have appeared in other magazines and in daily papers, each portraying a seductively-dressed girl, coyly "speaking" the advertising copy. Men admire the picture but the women readers appear to take the text seriously. One read:

> I'm in love again and that means being *alive!* Every morning I wake up feeling like strawberries in champagne! Wouldn't you suppose someone like me would *always* be in love? Well, there are people you love at all times . . . friends, mother and father, ex-beaux, animals . . . maybe a perfect glass-blue morning or your favorite recording star, but *in* love . . . well that's the fantastic *most* and only happens *once* in a while. My favorite magazine says one should love many different people but always be ready for that heady, ultimate experience. I love that magazine. They really understand my psyche. I guess you could say I'm That COSMOPOLITAN Girl.

To bolster the more daring content Mrs. Brown made other changes which readers must have noted, such as a more modern typographic design and sprucing up the tone of the titles of the articles.

Cosmopolitan, in other words, thanks to a shrewd, clever and tasteless editor, got itself all together, held on to some of its conventional content ("A Complete Handbook on the Care and Pampering of Your Skin—Whatever Your Problem"; "How to Diet—Successfully—on Five Meals a Day" and "All About Amsterdam.") but injected convention-defying material at the same time. It made enemies in the women's liberation movement, but may have profited from the publicity resulting from the attacks.

THE EDITORIAL PURPOSE

Regarding certain outstanding disasters in magazine publishing, it is possible to observe that well-meaning management sometimes was inexperienced in the business and seemed to think that fact unimportant—for example, the Crowell-Collier and Curtis failures. The important factor of a well-defined editorial purpose, however, has been given much too little emphasis when analyzing the events affecting the decline of magazine giants. Such an editorial purpose can, in fact, provide a defense against the stresses and strains of an uncertain economy for it builds loyalty to the publication on the part of both readers and advertisers—both of which undergird the magazine. Prime examples are *Sports Illustrated, Yachting, TV Guide* and *Woman's Day,* in addition to various periodicals of smaller but still substantial circulation serving specialties.

Whatever may be thought of *Playboy*—and whole books have been devoted to speculation about it—there is no doubt that its astonishing success has come about not just through luck or smart management. Hugh Hefner, its founder, selected a group of male readers as his target and gave that identifiable audience what it wanted. He not only watched that audi-

Reprinted with permission from *The Saturday Evening Post* © The Curtis Publishing Company. Cartoon by Ronald Reilly.

ence but devised a formula that created other readers as well. He mixed the off-color with the serious, egg-headish copy, engaged the best writers and artists and sold his readers to logical advertisers. That the definable purpose gave his management an easier job is shown by the failures of that same management with two other magazines lacking such a graspable aim: *Show Business Illustrated* and *Trump*. The first, begun in 1962, had little originality. Much of its reading matter was on hackneyed subjects, such as already well-publicized show-world personalities. A bi-weekly, it also aped various characteristics of *Playboy,* as well as some of its typography (not surprising since much of its production was by the *Playboy* staff). In a year it was sold to *Show,* a rival. *Trump,* a monthly, was an attempt at a "slick, new, full-color satire magazine," as Hefner described it, according to Joe Goldberg, *Playboy's* historian. The cemetery for American humor magazines is one of the most crowded final resting places in all magazine-dom. Various types of U.S. periodicals are 100 or more years old, but no humor periodical today is aching from old-age pains. *Trump,* despite its color printing and timely satire, lasted only two months, in 1957. In a highly competitive field it takes heavy promotion and hard work by all departments to make a go of a humor magazine. This one did not receive the attention it needed to give it the originality and clear purpose necessary for survival. *Mad,* or one of its numerous imitators, was enough for the market.

Similar experiences were encountered by Time Inc. with *Letters;* by Curtis with *TV Week;* by Esquire, Inc., with *Bridegroom;* McCall Corp. with *Better Living;* and many more by little firms whose ill-fated products' names are on the gravestones. In some instances the fault was in not defining the field, in others through mistakes of judgment; not a few stumbled for lack of background research in advance of publication, either as to the audience potential, the advertising market or the nature of the competition.

Such experiences by publishers create a credibility gap with the public and destroy advertiser confidence in the publications. So keen is the realization by the more alert industry leaders that the loss of credibility and confidence is serious that in recent years a few of them have been looking squarely at the situation. They have been speaking to management groups and to the advertising business at conventions or by publishing articles in the trade press. Now and then discussion of the problems finds its way into a consumer publication.

While he was editor of *Saturday Review,* for instance, Norman Cousins encouraged its Communications supplement editor to print discussion of what was happening to magazines. On the death of *Look,* Cousins spoke to his readers through his editorial in the main body of his publication. He pointed out, in "The Death of 'Look' " on Oct. 2, 1971, that television had replaced magazines as "the single most important medium of national communication" and went on to describe the effect of it on periodicals, compared their respective operating costs, and then, pointed up the inequity and damaging effect of the continuing rise in costs of mail distribution of magazines.

Always one to consider the readers of his magazines, Cousins concluded:

> Over the years, we haven't hesitated to speak to our readers about internal affairs at *SR*. We don't hesitate to speak now about a situation that was a major factor in the decision to discontinue *Look* magazine and that is very much on the minds of all those who have chosen periodical publishing as their profession.

The affected magazines have the problems discussed here. But they also have various other problems, such as those Norman Cousins may have had in mind and that readers may wish to understand more fully.

6

The
Problems Magazines Face

A READER'S MAIN relationship with the magazines he subscribes for or buys at newsstands is through their circulation departments. In spite of that, some magazine publishing firms put small fortunes into public relations departments but spend comparatively little money to improve their operations for dependably putting the publication before the readers' eyes. Some of the more severe headaches for management may result from this, although they are not new. Getting the publication to readers has created difficulties for publishers ever since the days, two centuries ago, when periodicals were read in New York or Philadelphia coffee houses, with one copy serving all patrons.

Obviously, for the majority of readers, the relationship of readers to circulation department is satisfactory, however, for if this were not so readers would ignore the publication. But enough of them, like Mr. and Ms. Mistrustful Reader we already have met, have their troubles with circulation to reveal to magazine publishers that there are serious problems in their distributing systems.

What reader, at some time or another, has not been billed twice for the same subscription or, more rarely, not at all? Who has not, now and then, received his copy with the cover torn, smudged or folded? Or found a strange magazine in his mailbox and missed one of his own? Or tried to buy a certain issue only to find out that the dealer: (1) has not yet received it, although it is long overdue; (2) ran out because his order is regularly too low; (3) discontinued it for what he considered lack of demand?

Publishers and their circulation departments know all about such experiences, of course. They are helplessly at the mercy of human failure, mechanical breakdowns, postal service requirements and inadequacies, the weather and the inability of the industry so far to devise an improved distribution system. Experiments go on with delivery via neighborhood newspaper boy, use of metal receptacles on the suburban and rural roads erected in front of subscribers' homes, delivery by private mail firms and even by the milkman, and sale from machines similar to those that disgorge paperbacks or candy. Thought is given as well to ways to keep dealers from allowing the high school kids and others to do their reading free at the drug store or supermarket racks, with the result that in an hour the magazines displayed are in a jumble—*Playboy* cheek-to-cheek with *House and Garden* and *Black Belt* upside down on *Weight Watchers*. On this problem the industry seems practically to have given up attempts to find a solution; it contents itself with experiments and doing what it can to keep the present service level from going lower.

For circulation is only one of many problems. The check-list of all those facing magazines these days—computerism, wobbly economics, restive youth, women and racial minorities, in short, a changing social order—is discouragingly long. Fortunately for the industry, scores of publishers either are unaware of them or are headstrongly indifferent or defiant. They go right on with planning and producing new magazines, most of which die after a few issues. But a number find a place of their own, some even rising to positions of social value or successful business operations that make their owners well-to-do (if nothing more).

THE WOULD-BE PUBLISHERS

A familiar scene in the author's offices in the several universities where he has been helping to prepare the young and some of the not-so-young for work in the magazine field has been repeated year in and year out since 1937, when he first engaged in magazine journalism education.

Usually by pre-arrangement one or two young men, or now and then a married couple, and rarely a young woman, appear at the office to discuss an idea for a new magazine. These eager beings would not think of going to a physician or a lawyer whom they do not know and asking for free diagnosis, prescriptions, counsel and guidance. But a university specialist is at everyone's service, it seems, like pastor, priest and rabbi. And thus it should be, if education is to be social in effect. The difference, of course, is that the religious are not often asked by their petitioners how to get rich.

This particular time the visitors are two recent graduates of an Ivy League university, one which does not deign to offer courses in communications. Both young men are strangers to the consultant. The conversation falls into the usual pattern, and on this occasion unfolded in more or less the usual way.

"So you are thinking of starting a new magazine? Tell me about it. And which of you is Luce and which Hadden?"

They grin. Sure, they know about Time Inc.'s founders. They rush into the description of their project together in their high enthusiasm, laugh, and then the major spokesman takes over. Soon he stops abruptly, having remembered something.

"We assume . . . uh . . . well . . . that we can tell you all this in confidence?"

He is assured he can. Evidently the pair knows the story of how Ben Franklin's aide spilled the news that Ben was planning a magazine, back in 1740. He snitched to Andrew Bradford, also a printer, and as a result Bradford's *American Magazine, or a Monthly View of the Political State of the British Colonies* was available early in 1741, three days before Franklin's *The General Magazine, and Historical Chronicle for All the British Plantations in America.*

"Do you think some of these big companies, if we showed our dummy and prospectus to them, would just say 'Sorry, good bye' and then steal the idea and bring the magazine out themselves?"

They are assured of the unlikelihood that the responsible firms they named would engage in such trickery. A further point, usually convincing with others, is added: "Publishers of major magazines usually don't do that sort of thing, even if it weren't dishonest, because magazine publishing is such a big gamble in any case." They are told about the owner who remarked that bringing out new magazines these days is as much a gamble as betting at the Hialeah race track.

Now less nervous, the neophytes unload thousands of words about their babies. We leaf through an attractive (but often impractical) dummy of a magazine that is far too costly to produce with their resources. The dummy is filled with simulated contributions from high-priced writers, artists and photographers, and with advertising the owners cannot hope to obtain unless the magazine is an instant success. Virtually every page is printed in full color.

"Now we'd like your opinion of our pro forma budget," says one, feeling around in his briefcase and then extending a glassine-covered, business-like tabulation.

But it only looks business-like, for it covers five years of anticipated income and expenses, all in vague figures. For promotion, for instance, $300,000 is allotted for the first year; by the fifth it gradually has sunk to $70,000, as if promotion were not a continuing high expense, although not necessarily as high as during the first year. A half-million is set down for salaries at first; the figure rises gratifyingly to $2,000,000 by the fifth year. Some questions are raised.

"Where do you allocate editorial expenses?"

"In . . . uh . . . that Miscellaneous item at the bottom: $300,000."
"And have you allowed for overhead, like taxes and insurance?"
"Oh sure. They're in the Miscellaneous, too."
"Depreciation?"
"In Miscellaneous."
"And how about circulation operations? About how much will they cost and how do you expect to handle those operations?"
"Those costs are under Promotion. We're not sure yet how to handle that side. What do you suggest?"
And so it goes—all vague and dreamy.

By the end of the second hour the dreamers have been confronted with some of the problems ahead, most of which they had not thought about. They included: Postal rate increases; rising printing costs; the crowded market; inflation; recession; television competition; ethical problems created by content (particularly in their plans for two new magazines); competitive salaries; deals in advertising sales; union pressures; attacks on publishing freedom; media rivals; flexibility of formula and format; staff relationships.

What is amazing is that at the end of the session, after talking about the problems, a few of these starry-eyed, would-be publishers eventually succeed with their ventures. But most never get beyond the dream state. Effective results come about under three circumstances, usually: if they abandon that dream for a few years to take small jobs on magazines and learn the business from within; if they take graduate work in journalism and communications and add a year or two of experience; or if they are lucky enough to find a young, experienced, and talented individual to be the key executive and an investor in the venture.

If readers are to have some concept of what faces owners, publishers and editors they need to be given a closer look at certain magazine problems, particularly those involving a significant investment of time, money, intellectual interest or social idealism. A few are examined here.

ATTACKS ON FREEDOM OF THE PRESS

Gaeton Fonzi, in his biography of Walter H. Annenberg, publisher of *TV Guide* and *Seventeen* magazines, one-time owner of the Philadelphia *Inquirer,* and in 1973 U.S. Ambassador to the Court of St. James's in London, tells a story of Annenberg's use of the *Inquirer* to retaliate for what Fonzi called "a backhanded slap at Annenberg." The statement objected to appeared in the December 1964 issue of *Holiday,* a Curtis monthly, then being published by the original Curtis firm.

"On the surface," said *Holiday,* "Walter Annenberg might seem to have everything against him as far as society is concerned." The Annenberg newspaper then published a series of articles declaring that Curtis was in serious financial trouble. Fonzi believes that "it was a rabbit punch to a company already on its knees."

Any experienced journalist knows of similar practices followed by other publications. The U.S. press is freer of such unethical uses of print than many another. But the publisher or editor who uses this magazine not only to even scores but also to further a point of view at the expense of the truth is no *rara avis* in this country. Such practices are factors in the continuing battle for freedom of the press or, as it is put by some warriors, the people's right to know.

Not many magazine readers think of policies promulgated by an owner or publisher as restraints on such a freedom or right. To the average reader, restrictions are those imposed by governments, through laws concerning censorship, obscenity, libel and so on. Spiro Agnew's speeches during his Vice Presidency in which he adversely criticized the media, singling out few magazines but mainly spotlighting certain newspapers and broadcasters, have been labelled by some critics as government interference or attempts at putting restraints upon the communications media.

Government attitudes and exercises of official powers are indeed part of the problem of attacks on press freedom that are faced by magazine owners and their staffs. They have been examined in detail by numerous scholars as well as working magazinists. This problem reached the height of attention, at least in recent years, in the case of the Pentagon Papers and was kept alive by later events, such as the exposés by Jack Anderson, the newspaper columnist. Sometimes, however, the situation is altered and a magazine toys with freedom. The *National Review,* for example, hoaxed many newspapers soon after the Pentagon Papers series appeared in the New York *Times* and other papers. The magazine ran a piece called "The Secret Papers They Didn't Publish," supposedly about classified documents leaked to the *Review,* allegedly 1962–66 memoranda. Stories based on the article appeared on many broadcasts and in newspapers. William F. Buckley, Jr., the *Review's* editor, later admitted the piece was a staff concoction, to show that "forged documents would be widely accepted" if they seemed plausible.

But actual government interference, an external force, is only part of the problem for magazine publishers. Another part is the internal interference with the "right to know" that some members of the publishing world practice on their readers, often inadvertently. Like all other humans, publishers are possessed of blind spots and unrecognized prejudices as well as capacities for deceiving readers. In citing the violations of press freedom that follow there is no assertion that they are common; they merely illustrate situations. The forms they take are many.

Telling only part of the truth may be inadvertent or deliberate. What is printed may all be correct. But it is not necessarily the *entire* story. Newsmagazines are prone to leave out part of the facts, since they must be so selective in content. A case in point: *Time* reported on a meeting of specialists. One sensational statement made at one of the many sessions by a speaker was emphasized. The reader knew only that much about what went on during the three days of deliberations, for the rest was ignored in the magazine's coverage; in the space allotted nothing more could have been said. What appeared was the truth, but the report was distorted. In the attempt to provide readable material writers will abstract some sensational or startling single episode, concentrate on that, and thus create a false impression. Throughout the country there are thousands of meetings, conventions, conferences and other gatherings. To cover and write up each thoroughly would not only be impossible but also a staggering bore to most readers.

Related to this practice is that of emphasizing only one point of view. Magazines can concentrate on the viewpoint held by their owners or editors, giving either no space or short shrift to any other opinion. Those of large circulation as well as obscure magazines alike follow this course. Such emphasis is understandable but the reader, in order to know all the facts and arguments on subjects of interest to him, must read several periodicals of different shades of opinion and compare what they print if he is to reach a balanced judgment—if that is possible even then. But this is often a difficult procedure. Rarely are the magazines of non-conformist opinion found on newsstands, for example, and in some parts of the country they are not available in libraries as well. Freedom to read is negated under such conditions.

For some years, to take another example, the *Reader's Digest* published articles attacking the World Council of Churches. These articles were challenged as biased and inaccurate, but no space for reply was given by the *Digest*. Since this magazine does not carry a "letters to the editor" section the alleged errors went uncorrected. Two of such articles appeared in the October and November 1971 issues, asserting that the Council supports "insurrection," "draft dodgers," and "deserters" in the United States and Africa and that it is Russian-dominated. Protests were so strong that the magazine's editors agreed to print rebuttal articles by writers selected by the Council, giving other views on the WCC's activities.

There was also *Newsweek's* cover of May 6, 1969, which included a picture, now a photo-journalistic classic, showing armed black men marching from a building. The only caption was "Universities Under the Gun." The story inside made clear several important facts: the marchers were Cornell University students, this was an isolated incident, the guns were not loaded, a cross had been burned earlier outside a black women's residence hall, and radio reports said that cars with armed whites were on the way to the campus. But since these background facts were not widely publicized by the press, anyone receiving the magazine or seeing it on a newsstand would assume that armed insurrection was rife on university campuses and that black students were ruling them with guns.

Cynical readers say they suspect magazines of kowtowing to their advertisers. In so large an industry one is sure to find some owners or managers who will take out material that may displease their advertisers; they are more likely, however, not to prepare it for publication to begin with. Instances of such bowing to advertisers are common, even in some of the most widely circulated magazines. Various reasons are advanced in justification: fear of libel suits, lack of substantiation for the allegations made in content critical of advertisers, insufficient background to keep the criticisms in perspective, and the like. Even more restrictive than such self-censorship, is an identification so close to the aims of advertisers that owners and publishers are unaware of the untold stories of anti-social business practices or the inherent danger of certain advertised products. In the 1960's, for example, several widely-known magazines discontinued publication of cigarette advertising. But the large majority continued to print such ads, despite the warnings from responsible sources about the effects of smoking upon health. These same magazines, however, draw the line elsewhere, as with hard-core pornography. But "elsewhere" spends much less advertising money than the tobacco industry.

Consumer reaction to pricing, packaging, labeling and selling methods of the food industry, as well as manufacturers of other products, has been stepped up in recent years. Magazine treatment of this reaction has varied. The people's "right to know" has suffered in some instances because certain magazines fail to report official pronouncements or developments that may put various advertisers in a bad light.

A notable instance has been reported by A. Q. Mowbray, author of articles and books on the business practices of the food industry. He described in *The Nation* the relationships of the grocery trade associations and mass circulation magazines. Association officials meet with publishers to seek their cooperation on printing or not printing certain materials. He cites an instance during the 1960's when one official asked publishers to consider printing "some favorable articles about the food industry instead of only singling out cases of isolated criticism"; the words are attributed by Mowbray to Paul S. Willis, then president of the Grocery Manufacturers Association of America. Mowbray reported further that subsequently two articles on the Hart bill dealing with fair packaging and labeling never were used, although they had been commissioned by magazines. He checked directly with nine of the larger periodicals and learned that they "had told their readers nothing about the legislation that could have major implications for the prices paid in the supermarket." *Look* carried an article in

1965 attacking the bill, written by a General Foods official. The same book also bought space in other periodicals to call attention to the article, so it would have more influence. A chance to reply was requested by Senator Philip A. Hart, the bill's sponsor, but not granted. The extent to which *Look* engaged in such practices may have been a factor in its demise six years later.

Senator Hart at the same time sent background material on the bill to 21 magazines, with the idea that it would suggest articles or editorial comment. None of the 9 consumer and 12 grocery magazines published articles as a result. Mowbray's comment was that the publishers and editors had knuckled under from advertising pressure. The right of the public to know, in other words, had been ignored.

For years it was thought that what you don't know won't hurt you. Today the view is growing that it *will*. As a result, publication of muckraking and exposé material has been revived on a greater scale than any time since the days of Ida Tarbell and Upton Sinclair.

Ownership by one person or group of a large number of publications is a factor in freedom of the press usually discussed in connection with newspapers. Since the early days of William Randolph Hearst, Sr. and his large chain, down to today, ownership of many papers has become common. Among the principal newspaper chain or group owners are Newhouse, Scripps-Howard, Knight, The New York Times Co., Donrey Media, Scripps League, Dow-Jones, Gannett, Thomson, and Copley. Numerous others have smaller groups of dailies or substantial numbers of weeklies.

Several of these firms also own assemblies of magazines. Newhouse is reported to have 20, Dow-Jones more than a dozen, the New York Times Co. runs a half-dozen sports and medical periodicals as well as the multi-million circulation *Family Circle*. Add to these the holdings of McGraw-Hill, Johnson, Curtis, Downe and some less-widely known firms and this aspect of freedom of the press becomes an important part of the problem of maintaining the right to know. (See App. 6.)

In all fairness, however, the merits of controlling groups of magazines should be realized by readers. But these are advantages to the business interests concerned and not necessarily to the consumer supposedly served by these publications.

There may be safety in numbers, however. A firm with its whole future invested in one magazine is running a greater risk than does the firm with a variety of periodicals. Where such diversification exists, there is the possibility of sustaining a losing magazine by profits from others. *Look, Life* and *The Saturday Evening Post* were saved for a time in that way. But the one-magazine company, unless it has income from non-publishing enterprises, may be knocked out of business.

The group type of magazine ownership enables the company not only to absorb losses but also to use their other magazines as promotion media. *Ebony,* for example, is a successful magazine so strong that it has been able to crush several rivals in recent years; all, in fact, except *Sepia,* which itself is one of a group of five. Numerous highly specialized magazines have sent poachers to the graveyard or kept them in a minor place: *Boy's Life, Chain Store Age, American Heritage* and *Advertising Age* are examples.

Further, the publishing of several magazines by one owner permits lower costs of production for each. Space can be sold as combinations in all or several at a lower rate than the advertiser would have to pay if each magazine were independent. Similarly, certain editorial content can be used unchanged in two or more magazines in a group. One of the most common economies is that of giving staff members responsibilities on several books at a time. If these are the type of magazines that devote much space to news, the editorial department can gather the news items for more than one, as does McGraw-Hill for its numerous business and technical journals.

There are also tax advantages in corporate group ownership, such as on taxes in capital gains transactions involving the purchase or sale of a magazine property. And there is the correlated advantage of investment credit. Thus more sums are available for improving the business, increasing in that way the sales value at a later time. The accumulation of such low-tax dollars enables the owner of a magazine firm to use cash for buying other magazine properties. And that in itself is a more advantageous policy than borrowing to make payment for what may be a money-losing magazine at the time.

Depreciation rates also figure in the situation. A company that owns equipment (few firms own printing and other such heavy production machinery, for they contract with printers to have the work done) such as computerized office machines, mobile air-conditioners and automated projection units can write off such improvements on a rapid enough schedule to benefit under present tax laws. These benefits are more useful to a group-magazine owner than to a publisher of only one magazine.

In addition, overhead is lower. Little space need be used on this fact. Printing, payroll, insurance premiums, paper costs, rents, upkeep and various fixed charges are lower for a joint operation than for a number of single ones.

Giving the Reader What He Wants

Determining what a magazine's reading public wants and keeping its readers "loyal" are twin problems that must be faced by publishing management. A pragmatic view of this was expressed by Howard Allaway, while editor of *Popular Science Monthly* in the late 1950's and early 1960's, speaking at the University of Nebraska:

> Publishing is a business. Sure, we want to save the world; but the first responsibility of any magazine or newspaper is to survive, to stay alive, to come out again tomorrow or next month. If we can't do that, certainly we can't help to save the world. And to survive, any publisher must print enough of what some public wants, whether his public is a selected magazine audience or the whole population of a one-newspaper town. He must print enough of what some public wants to win and hold enough buyers and through them enough advertisers to pay the printing bills, to meet the payroll, and have a little left over.
>
> Obviously, we can't survive as editors by airily printing only what we happen to like, or trying to force on our readers only what we think they ought to have. Picture your prospective reader. There he sits in his chair after supper about to read, but he's drowsy from eating too much. Outside a dog is barking, and from the next room the kids' radio drills a singing commercial into his ear. He keeps remembering he ought to mend the backdoor screen. And he picks up your newspaper or my magazine, and he dares us to get him interested and to keep him reading. Our readers are not a captive audience, even in a one-newspaper town. They are free to take us or leave us alone, and they will leave us alone in droves unless we give them at least their seven cents' or thirty-five cents' worth of what they want along with whatever else we give them.

Once again *The Saturday Evening Post,* original Curtis model, provides an example. The magazine coasted along for years giving the public what the editors *thought* the public, or at least what its particular readership, wanted. It turned out that only a part of the public demanded old fashioned content—short stories of little depth, innumerable articles devoted to someone's personal success, and editorials upholding by then archaic political and social views. So in time so much of the reading public turned away that the editors could not stage enough of a recovery to save the *Post* as a multi-million circulation magazine.

In attempting to solve such problems, publishers have tried "reader interest studies." While useful as weathervanes, they still do not provide sound editorial formulas for several reasons: (1) Many people who answer the survey questions want to be regarded as liking certain kinds of material but actually may not as much as they say they do. (2) Readers really cannot be depended on to know what they like except over the long run. Tonight, during an interview, they indicate their liking for certain features. But a week from today, they might not read a similar article or story because they may feel different emotionally or the piece may seem repetitious (which it actually may be in its essentials). (3) They may be busy, worried, angry, sluggish, hungry, or impatient at the time of the survey and therefore give inaccurate responses. In fact, for a magazine to give the reader what he says he wants, over and over, will indeed pale after a while unless that reader is one of those limited intellects content to absorb the same fare, more or less, year after year. There are many such, of course, but whether a magazine can bet its future on them is debatable.

Prize contests are even less dependable as barometers than surveys, as publishers have discovered. Readers can be found who will say in a letter that they like a certain magazine feature because the lure of a possible prize will convince them that they admire it.

So no dependable yardstick has been found, neither those mentioned nor others not described. And those devices used so far tend to work an injustice on the content. Suppose, for example, that a certain comic cartoon or regular humorous column is left out of an issue. Readers are heard from in a chorus of objection. Let us also suppose that a certain column, perhaps one on the arts, is omitted for two months running. Little complaint follows. The magazine editor knows well enough that humorous material has many loyal readers and that, except in magazines of the arts or the few general periodicals that take art comment and criticism seriously, readers about such subjects are relatively few. These editors are tempted then to drop the art column as having too little following, thereby depriving readers of possibly valuable material and the magazine of that much usefulness and distinction.

Changes of Format and Formula

Even people in the publishing world confuse *format* and *formula*. The first has to do with the physical aspects of a magazine. Its format is what the publication looks like: its over-all dimensions, typography, layout, cover designs, and the sequence of such elements as the contents page, advertising, articles, stories and other content. The formula is the basic motif, the approach or the philosophical concept of the magazine's management of what it wants the magazine to stand for, what theme and purpose it is to have, what ideas are to be kept in focus. Two magazines that have basically similar formats but different formulas are, for example, *National Review* and *The Nation*.

Maintaining both successful formats and formulas are on-going problems of publishing, the first governed largely by capital and profits, the second controlled by a variety of factors. Money can buy handsome design and top-notch printing but knowledge of the reading public, appreciation of suitable writers and illustrators, imagination and the capacity to produce original over-all concepts are not primarily dollars-and-cents matters. The distinctive and often successful magazines in this country's history were reflections of men and women with a genius for publishing or editing. When H.L. Mencken and George Jean Nathan put their heads together a revamped *Smart Set* resulted. From it developed *The American Mercury,* which Alfred Knopf launched in 1924, with Mencken and Nathan as editors. Its formula was theirs, however. Harold Ross conceived of *The New Yorker;* DeWitt Wallace dreamed up *Reader's Digest.* Norman Cousins moulded *Saturday Review* along the lines of his idea for a magazine of literary and public affairs topics.

Behind every original formula are one or more persons with ideas of what a magazine for a particular purpose should say and stand for. Format, if handled properly, carries out the formula physically. Thus sports magazines use bold typography, to represent the vigor and ruggedness of athletic life, and presumably of the actual or vicariously exercising readers. Despite the liberation movement, some women's magazines continue to select delicate, feminine typefaces to represent female fragility and tenderness. The rock culture is reflected in that movement's journalism in different ways as the supporters change their life styles—psychedelic at times, back-to-mother-earth at others.

CHANGES IN PUBLIC TASTE

From time to time the United States is swept by interests, fads and movements that create problems for magazines. In the 1960's and early 1970's we have seen such movements as the Jesus Freaks, who have been described as religious fundamentalists in long hair and messy clothes; the women's liberation movement (the National Organization for Women and numerous other formal groups within it) which has revived some aspects of the days of Susan B. Anthony and Elizabeth Stanton Cady; the rise of countless ethnic group associations, such as the Congress of Racial Equality and the Nation of Islam, and like bodies for American Indians, Mexican-Americans, Chinese-Americans and Cubans, among others; and the organized homosexuals, through the Gay Liberation movement. These and other more obvious social groupings, such as the political revolutionaries and counter-revolutionaries of both sexes and all races, and the groups to improve the ecology or support conservation or consumerism or oppose the American presence in Indochina, have introduced into old magazines and new ones reflections of these special interests.

As a consequence, some topics once untouched by popular magazines are common today. We now see articles discussing "The Consequences of Consumerism in Our Schools," "He and She: The Sex Hormones and Behavior," and "Every Girl Needs—A Supportive Man."

It is not that American public taste comes from a united population all of a single mind, as the rulers of totalitarian countries seem to think about their citizens. The taste of the U.S. public is segmented—fortunately so for the specialized magazines, which therefore can appeal to various categories, but not so fortunate for the consumer books, which must avoid alienating too many such segments at one time.

The problems of magazines are closely parallel to their faults, for certain of the difficulties stem from those faults. Thus far it may have seemed to readers of this book that the industry is producing magazines beset by troubles and deficient in virtues. The troubles exist for all, for no human institution lacks them, but the scorecard on faults and virtues is not as unbalanced as it may seem.

7

The Faults and Virtues

WRITERS SEEKING TO evaluate the performance of the mass media have focused almost entirely upon newspaper publishing and radio-television broadcasting, but little more than scattered articles and a few books have been devoted to magazine publishing.

The reasons for neglecting magazines are several and clear enough. Traditionally the periodical has been thought to be little more than a bit of entertainment or a personal guidebook. Only in recent years have many gone beyond those functions, although there was a time in the days of the muckrakers early in this century when some of the largest and most popular raked plenty of muck and caused readers to think. But the rakes were stored in the barn again, after a while, as public interest in exposés of corruption in official circles or debunking public heroes waned. With movements like those kept alive by Nader's Raiders, muckraking returned in strength in the 1960's and 1970's. On the other hand, newspapers were founded in this country a half century before magazines so, earlier, they were journalistic leaders and more influential. They were, and still are, published more frequently than magazines, by and large, and therefore have more immediate contact with the public. Papers also have cost less per copy, and seemed the less expensive, although on an annual basis the outlay is far greater.

Television has been subjected to sharp analysis because of what it has purveyed, some of which has aroused special social concern, notably the portrayal of violence. Both television and radio broadcasting have been accused of domination by advertisers. Newspapers and magazines have been so accused, also. But with broadcasts nothing else is on the air or

75

screen when commercials appear, whereas printed pages share space with
editorial copy—except for full-page ads and even so these usually are opposite reading matter.

The few, skimpy appraisals of U.S. magazine performance are in
chapters of a handful of books and in occasional articles. These have been
mild compared with the book-length criticisms of newspapers, most all
of which, beginning in 1859 with Lambert Wilmer's *Our Press Gang* down
to the volumes of the 1970's by James Aronson and Ben Bagdikian, have
been basically unfavorable reactions. Few volumes are concerned with
the virtues of the press, perhaps because it is easier to write a condemna-
tory book—and readers seem to respond more enthusiastically to such
books.

Someone who has worked all day is not in a mood to dissect magazines during an evening's leisure time although that reader may damn one
if it carries news he considers bad, tending to blame the messenger for the
message. He (or she) also may denounce another publication for its
opinions if he disagrees, but this reaction usually is not so much analysis as
emotion. In fact, attracted as so many Americans are to television watching, only the more earnest ponder about what is right or wrong about
any printed journalistic medium. Just how many ponderers there may be is
difficult, probably impossible, to say. Statistics on circulation and library
use are relatively clear but hardly are enough evidence on which to base
even an estimate.

READERS' VIEWS—AN IMAGINARY SYMPOSIUM

A mythical symposium on the pros and cons of magazine performance
might suggest some public opinion on magazines. It could be along the
lines of what follows.

Let us assume that the panelists are two editors and two readers,
presided over by a moderator. The editors are Miss Lesley Alden, of
"Family Day," a monthly for houswives, and Richard Robins, editor of
"Black Life," a consumer periodical for black citizens. The readers are
John Pitts, an accountant, and Mrs. Sara Miller, a housewife. The moderator is Professor Raymond Eng, head of the communications department
at Atlantis University in California. The occasion, part of the program of
the spring session of the Magazine Industry Colloquium at the Green House
Inn, near Bath, Maine. After introducing the panel members, the moderator describes the situation.

ENG: Since the magazine business has no ombudsmen the panel has agreed
to discuss the pros and cons of the business without attempting to reach a
conclusion about whether it is mainly full of virtues or chiefly filled with
faults. Mrs. Miller, will you start us off? You are a housewife. What would

you say is the outstanding fault or virtue of our magazines? In your opinion, that is.

MRS. MILLER: I think it depends on what kind of magazines you are talking about, doctor. I don't think it's fair to lump all magazines together. I read or see several for women and we have lots of others around the house: *Sea* and *The Rotarian* and *Camping* and I don't know what else for my husband. The girl gets *Seventeen* and the boy gets a scout one. And our church sends one. So how can I say something that fits all these different ones?

PITTS: If Mrs. Miller can't, I can.

ENG: Go ahead.

PITTS: Almost all American magazines, especially most of these big ones like the women's and the newsmagazines, are just greedy money-makers —or trying to be money-makers. Maybe that church magazine and a few others that are paid for by their organizations aren't so commercial. But the rest are for sure.

MISS ALDEN: Even *The Rotarian?*

PITTS: Especially that one, I'd say. All it does is bless the social order under which its readers thrive. All those luncheon club magazines just reflect the business world in which the members move, trying to get each others' business.

MRS. MILLER: But look at all the good those Rotary organizations do. They raise money for scholarships, they help improve neighborhoods, and they support a lot of other good causes.

PITTS: Sure, and have been for years, haven't they? But what have they done about race prejudice until recent years? Have they opposed? Have they spoken out for anti-gun legislation, for example?

ROBINS: I agree with Mr. Pitts, there. One reason there is such a magazine as mine is that the general ones weren't doing much to correct the failure to give us black people full civil rights. The regular press just ignored us or printed only what made us all seem to be criminals or fools.

ENG: Miss Alden, do you think Mr. Robins' point is valid?

MISS ALDEN: I'm afraid I do, although he seems to imply it was a deliberate conspiracy by white editors and publishers. There were reasons why the black people of this country were not thought of as part of the audience. And maybe other minority groups, too. Maybe this was because of their poverty and having no education . . .

PITTS: You mean inability to get a decent education because of discrimination.

MISS ALDEN: You could put it that way, if you want. But conditions are changing and with I don't know how many Negroes in this country, millions and millions. . . .

PITTS: About 23 millions. Right, Robins?

ROBINS: Right. More than the whole population of Canada.

MISS ALDEN: So I think white publishers are beginning to realize that's a large potential readership, especially since the educational level is on the way up.

PITTS: And a big market for advertisers, too, don't forget. Another thing we shouldn't forget is that magazine publishers don't have to face any of the government-imposed restraints that face radio and television. No magazine owner has to apply every three years to the government for permission to continue printing. His magazine isn't under demand from some commission or other to justify what he has printed. He has freedom from that kind of regulation. These magazine owners benefit from the First Amendment to the Constitution, but far too many seem not to realize it and don't take advantage of it by operating more fully in the public interest.

ENG: That's true, and there's another important aspect I'd like to interject here. It grows out of what you've just been saying, Mr. Pitts. I see a lot of magazines that speak out on various social issues. It seems to me that the public is being exposed to new ideas all the time.

PITTS: If you're thinking of a few like *The Progressive* or *Ramparts,* you're right. Although some of that group has been debunking the frauds and poltroons in our society for years. The *New Republic* is more than 50 years old and *The Churchman* more than 100.

ENG: Still you can find more concern about social issues in the big magazines, too, than we've seen in many years—like environment and the ecology.

MISS ALDEN: And the rights of women and consumerism and the drug traffic. All kinds of magazines are fighting those battles and a lot of others.

ENG: Are we agreed, then, that a good many magazines are doing something useful for society?

PITTS: I'd agree they're doing something useful, sure. Let's hope. But I'd have to add that it's not enough when you think of the emergencies. Here scientists are predicting that it won't be too many more years before we'll be inundated by our own garbage. Or that we'll have so ruined our waterways that there'll be no fresh water any more.

ENG: What about the encouragement to literature and the arts? Aren't magazines doing that? They used to.

ROBINS: I read something not long ago about two publishers starting a new magazine of fiction because so few magazines print stories any more. That doesn't sound like much literary progress to me.

MRS. MILLER: Right here I'd like to say something. Maybe the world's greatest literature isn't being published but the magazines that come into my home are doing a lot to help people live better. Maybe even longer. They're interested in adopting orphans and caring for underprivileged kids.

Think of all they have done for years about personal hygiene, cleanliness in the home and the beauty of every day living. It's amazing.

MISS ALDEN: Glad to hear you say that, Mrs. Miller. A lot of people take all that for granted. There was a time in this country when people brushed their teeth with twigs and we had no sewer system. Magazines like mine have done a lot for improvement and solving marriage problems, for proper child care and treatment of the sick, for example.

ROBINS: That's what we're trying to do at my shop for our readers. We still can do something you don't or can't do—pitch that sort of help in the right direction.

PITTS: There's another side to that coin, ladies and gentlemen. Some magazines do all those things you're talking about—if it pays them and if they can sell advertising to go along with it.

MISS ALDEN: Don't be so cynical. We have to survive, remember.

PITTS: I don't see why. Why do we have to have so many magazines? Aren't the mails and the newsstands too crowded as it is? Anyway, let me go back to what I was saying. The really bad thing magazines do is push a lot of people into spending their money on things they really don't need. Not only obvious things like fancy foods and drinks and cosmetics. But also expensive houses and furniture and extra cars and high-priced cameras and a lot of other showy things.

ENG: Since no one wants to take up that one I wonder if we could discuss further the point about the magazines' contribution to literature and other arts. Shouldn't we explore that a bit more? When you stop to think of it, here are many famous writers and artists who got their start in magazines. You can go as far back as Poe and Holmes and Howells. Later on Hemingway and Fitzgerald. Today it's John Hersey and Flannery O'Connor and John Updike and Eudora Welty. John Hawkes and Philip Roth first appeared in the little literary magazines. The best non-fiction is in today's magazines, also.

PITTS: Like whose?

ENG: Would you accept E. B. White? George Elliott? James Baldwin? Norman Mailer? Truman Capote?

PITTS: Mailer, yes. Capote, no.

MISS ALDEN: Don't forget Tom Wolfe.

PITTS: That punctuation-slinger! Are you kidding?

ENG: Well, I think that, by and large, we must admit that the magazines have done a lot for writers. Some have even supported them for years until they were successful.

PITTS: Earlier you included the arts. Big magazines usually have been obstructionist when it comes to the arts, printing cartoons that make fun of the more advanced artists, like the abstractionists. They give the public the idea that the traditionalists are the only true artists.

ROBINS: I'm afraid I agree that that's true, Dr. Eng. Sure, a few art magazines have been open-minded. But the general ones haven't done much to explain the place of experimental art.

PITTS: Or music, for that matter.

ENG: I have received the signal, ladies and gentlemen, that it is time for us to allow questions from the audience. Would someone then like to address a question to the panel in general or any one of the panelists in particular? . . . . Yes, that gentleman on the left . . .

QUESTIONER: It seems to me that a lot of the big magazines these days have declared war on business. I don't see why advertisers should support such consumerist magazines as *Good Housekeeping, Parents, Ladies' Home Journal* and *Reader's Digest.* . . .

PITTS: Did he really call them consumerist magazines? My God. I can't believe he really reads them.

QUESTIONER: . . . How does the panel justify expecting business people to support magazines that are out to hurt them?

MISS ALDEN: May I deal with that question, doctor? I think the justification is that our duty first of all is to our readers. The consumer movement is increasingly powerful. If we are to hold the respect of our readers we must look out for their interests. Another justification is that enlightened business people are concerned about high quality, reasonable prices, dependable service and the other things the consumer advocates are worried about. They want public confidence, too.

PITTS: I'd like to add something to that, if I may. I don't see those particular magazines the gentleman mentioned as particularly consumer-minded. There are some that do, like Consumer's Union *Reports,* and some others give space to such material. They and some others that are opposing pollution, war and other social evils are a credit to the magazine business, especially if it is at the expense of advertising money. A lot of 'em weren't that way back in the 1960's.

QUESTIONER: This panel is supposed to be dealing with the faults and virtues of magazines. But so far I've heard nothing about the way magazines constantly picture women as sex objects and second-class citizens. They deal almost entirely with their appearance, their sex lure power, or their kitchen prowess. Is this a virtue or a fault? I can tell you it's a fault in my book.

MISS ALDEN: I think the lady is over-simplifying the matter. There's a group of women in this country who think all women think as they do. I have in mind such people as Kate Millett, Florynce Kennedy and Caroline Bird. Or those who descended on the offices of the *Ladies' Home Journal* and *Cosmopolitan,* protesting what they called "the sexual exploitation of women." I contend that most women in this country—and that includes most readers of women's magazines—don't consider themselves exploited in any way. You can't expect the magazines to change their basic content just to please a small minority. It just isn't reasonable. In fact, it's a form of publishing suicide.

PITTS: I'd like Miss Alden to tell me how she knows how many women think which way about that?

MISS ALDEN: At my office we judge by the mail we get. And it's overwhelmingly against the school of thought represented by Betty Frieden, Gloria Steinem & Co. And we've talked to the editors of other magazines, the ones like ours: *Woman's Day* and *Family Circle*. They have the same experience. I have tried putting in a little material along the lines of the women's lib philosophy. And lots of our readers, and you know we have quite a few millions of them, do almost nothing except protest when we use it.

OTHER MAGAZINE PROS AND CONS

The discussion ended on that viewpoint. Like most such sessions, it had covered only a few of the pros and cons that should be dealt with in a more thorough review. Here are some important additional ones that could have been taken up at another session.

Editorial Carelessness (Con)

After hearing about certain incidents that have occurred in the early 1970's, readers must believe there is considerable editorial carelessness in magazine offices. The Clifford Irving-Howard Hughes affair created considerable skepticism about magazine content dependability, at least among thoughtful readers. For years Time Inc. had described proudly its system of checking its various magazines' copy. But in handling the Irving material, it gave the world an appalling demonstration of slovenly editing, as had *The Saturday Evening Post* some years before in publishing an article which concerned a telephone conversation between two football-team coaches. It led to legal suits against the publishing house by each coach, asking for a total of $20-million in damages. When the suits were settled the total had been reduced to $760,000—still a sum that would wipe out a smaller firm.

The attitude at Time Inc. about the Irving-Hughes matter was revealed by Donald Wilson, then corporate vice president, as quoted by Stephen Isaacs, of the Washington *Post,* in the *Columbia Journalism Review*. Isaacs reported that he had asked Wilson, when the deception first began, how he was so sure that the book was "the real item," as Wilson had called it.

"Oh, we're absolutely positive," he said. "Look, we're dealing with people like McGraw-Hill. And, you know, we're not exactly a movie magazine. This is Time Inc. and McGraw-Hill talking. We've checked this thing out. We have proof."

Bucinator, the pen name of a *Harper* contributor, pointed out that this time was not the first that Time Inc. had tried what he called "secret journalism." He recalled the instance of the Khrushchev memoirs, which *Life* published. The book, *Khrushchev Remembers,* was compiled from various sources and not written by the Soviet leader as a book, was released without his knowledge and approval, and later was found to be guilty of "known and flagrant inaccuracies," as Bucinator put it. He (or perhaps it was a she) concluded:

> Finally, of course, what does secret journalism produce as journalism? Isn't it the ethic and essence of journalism not to cover up but to open up, expose, reveal, and publicize? A mood, a moral climate, seems to have been changing; it is no longer easy for those who observe *Life* and *Time* to be sure what they would do with something like the Pentagon Papers or the Anderson Papers, or the Peers Inquiry Report on the Army cover-up of the My Lai massacres that Seymour Hersh broke in *The New Yorker.*

Nat Hentoff, a free-lancer for many magazines and newspapers, turned up another and different example of editorial carelessness. It was committed by the respected magazine of public affairs, *Commentary,* and a group of other publications subsequently. In its December 1971, issue *Commentary* published an article by Professor Joseph Bishop of Yale Law School called "Politics & ACLU." It was a brief against the American Civil Liberties Union. Hentoff discovered numerous errors and distortions which were printed by the magazine without checking.

The Washington *Evening Star* reprinted the entire article; Hentoff asserts that the errors were compounded thereby. Then the *Wall Street Journal* devoted its lead editorial to it, accepting statements without checking. The *Journal* editorial was echoed in the Lancaster (Pa.) *New Era,* the Philadelphia *Inquirer,* WSOC, a Charlotte (N.C.) radio station, and by a number of columnists such as Jeffrey St. John, William F. Buckley, Jr., Victor Lasky, and others identified consistently with conservative political and social philosophies.

The list of errors and distortions compiled by Aryeh Neier, executive director of the ACLU, is far too long to reproduce here; *Commentary's* editors were sufficiently impressed to print the rebuttal in a later issue. A sample of the errors may suffice here. The original article said that the ACLU does not defend right wingers. The Union produced ample evidence that it had done so within the preceding year, aiding the Ku Klux Klan, the John Birch Society, the White Power movement and ten more of this type.

The Quality of Fiction (Con)

Another contrary or adversely critical view of magazines concerns the falsity of so much of its fiction. Although the quality has improved in some magazines in recent years, by and large it is low-quality fiction that appears in the vast majority of periodicals that still carry such stuff of the authorial imagination. And in those books that have been known for the high quality of much of their fiction, the quantity has decreased sharply. Some of the most important serious outlets for fiction have cut it out entirely—*Harper's Bazaar,* for example. Others have reduced it 50 or 75 per cent (*Atlantic* and *Harper's*). And what appears still plentifully in the low-cost fan-, confession-, romance-, adventure-, sex- and other widely-read magazines is more typical of the total fiction fare than what is in the handful of magazines still printing serious fiction. An astonishingly astute statement of the distaste of some readers for magazine fiction was expressed in 1970 by Blaze Starr, the red-haired "Queen of Burlesque," as she was being billed in the late 1960's. She is reported to have told George Malko, in *Lithopinion:*

> I don't believe anything I read, especially, of, my God, a lot of these magazines. Most of 'em . . . it's funny. Somebody will sit and dream up a wild, wild and way out beautiful story that never really happened to anybody. And they make it end beautifully. And everybody reads it and everybody loves it, and then somebody buys it, and somebody makes a movie, and all these people living through this phony world that somebody dreamed up in the first place. 'Cause in real life things don't turn out like that.

Magazine fiction falls into two groups: the literary, printed and read by only a few; and the unliterary, printed and read by the many. The loss of it or changes in it in certain magazines has meant that most readers no longer look to magazines for quality fiction. Television and paperback books are factors in these attitudes as much as editorial decisions. But magazine editors are aware of the attitudes of their publics and choose their content accordingly. Hit by bad times, the literary magazines, big and little, are less of an outlet than they used to be.

News in Perspective (Pro)

Henry A. Grunwald, managing editor of *Time,* while being interviewed on television in 1971 by Edwin Newman, described what some magazines have contributed to readers for years, but today perhaps more than ever because needed more than ever. "The printed media," he said, "organized the unorganized." Newsmagazines, he observed with natural loyalty to his own, help the public to see the pattern of the news. He could have added that they also help the reader at least to see *a* pattern. *The* pattern is not so easy to discern, and what is discerned is not necessarily accurate just because the various newsmagazines seek to shape the news in their individual ways. They do not, by any means, always agree. Yet magazines, more so than newspapers, be they newsmagazines or other kinds with news in them, do show possible relationships that help confused readers make some sense of what is going on—if any sense can be made of some events these days. Grunwald acknowledged that television has made the newsmagazine "tie the picture together and show the meaning of the bits," as he put it.

At first it was the newspapers that pushed these magazines into the procedure of binding the news bundles. Other periodicals, it should be observed, are doing even more than that to put the news in perspective. The newsweeklies attempt to cover a large area with relatively concise and brief articles. But most in-depth presentation and interpretation is left to such periodicals as *Foreign Affairs, Center,* the *Atlantic, Yale Review* and *Vista.* Published less often, these and others like them have the time to do more thorough research and writing in the effort to pull everything together.

Contributions of the Business Publications (Pro)

Obviously some of the about 2,700 trade journals, most of which are magazines, are what A. Kent MacDougall, writing in the *Wall Street Journal,* once called "biased and bland." It would be extraordinary, in the existing social scheme, if a large number were otherwise, for these magazines are perhaps more dependent upon the prevailing order than even the consumer periodicals (some of which thrive without reliance upon advertising). But to give full credit to this big segment of the specialized magazines, they appear to be developing within their circle members that have additional aims than survival or making money out of the system.

The usual charges against these business publications, as they prefer to be called (since many have no connections with a trade), are that they publish advertising matter disguised as editorial material; that they wink at unethical practices in the businesses they report upon; that they are mere servants of those industries; that they give their advertisers a break in their editorial columns by mentioning them and their products favorably always; that editors too often sell the advertising space as well as supervise the editorial department. The business recession of the late 1960's and early 1970's, during which the volume of advertising in these publications as a whole fell and numbers of magazines failed, did not make it easier to overcome these accusations.

On the other hand, strong stands are taken from time to time by some of the higher quality periodicals of the business group, most of which are to be found in the membership list of the American Business Press, Inc., a trade organization for this segment of magazine journalism. But only about one-fifth of the total of such publications is affiliated with ABP. And it is the other four-fifths that shelter an unknown number that follow low ethical standards.

Details about certain of these vigorous positions, doing honor to the image of the business magazines, came out at the 1970 and 1971 editorial clinics of the ABP in New York and Chicago. Robert Kelsey, editor of *Modern Packaging,* described what his magazine did during its campaign against certain industry and association practices or policies that increase pollution. The 50 articles and editorials published in the drive were aimed at readers who also were advertisers. But retaliation did not follow. It did come, however, when an economic series showed a breakdown in packaging costs, he said. Advertisers called back between 20 and 30 pages. The periodical's efforts, nevertheless, were followed by a crusade for what he called "environmental responsibility." Believing that the magazine's materials are not enough, Kelsey explained that he relied on other activities as well to bring about changes in industry thinking and policies, such as speaking engagements, broadcasting appearances and promotion.

Cortland Gray Smith, editor of *Better Editing,* an ABP quarterly, in reporting on these editorial clinics also quoted the experiences related by editors of *Aviation Week, Engineering News-Record, Medical Economics* and *Sales Management* magazines in exposing industries' and an individual firm's mistakes or anti-social practices. These examples do not deny the existence of too many questionable publishing actions but simply are on the credit side of the ledger and an encouragement to other editors to take firm positions.

Fewer Objections to Advertising (Pro)

Although complaints about magazine advertising are frequent, compared with other media advertising, it appears to be less objectionable to the public. Warwick & Legler, an agency, in 1972 surveyed 5,000 men and women to determine their reactions toward advertising. It learned that 69% believe that much of the criticism is justified. Yet 96% of the respondents thought advertising wholly necessary.

Magazine Advertising, a newsletter published by the Magazine Publishers Association, reported about the same time, however, that the survey brought out the fact that magazines stood first in the favorable attitudes and last in the unfavorable. The media were rated on a scale of one to five. On all three favorable scores—"enjoyable," "informative," and "believable"—periodicals stood first with 3.8. Newspapers were next with 3.0; television followed, 2.6; radio 2.5; outdoor 2.1; and mail, 1.4. When asked which medium was regarded unfavorably the order was almost exactly reversed.

THE CHALLENGE FOR EDITORS AND PUBLISHERS

As with all other institutions designed by humans, the magazine business is neither all good nor all bad, and never will be all of either. The weight or influence of magazine performance is difficult to measure, especially if it be over-all. In view of the technological forces for change and the differing ways in which people use the media—such as getting the news via radio in cars, on beaches and in boats—it may behoove magazine management to be more than ever concerned about what magazines stand for in the public mind. It is not enough, as a few have done in recent years, to try to assure readers by being agreeable—at least to the olfactory sense—by using chemically-treated ink smelling like a pine forest, root beer or cigarettes.

It takes hard thinking about what obtains and holds public confidence. That involves a serious regard for the readers' viewpoint, an attempt to determine it by thorough research and a management identification with the readers that stops short by merely giving them what they want just because they seem to want it.

Management's position is perhaps delineated in an incident that occurred when Charles Morton, later a staff editor of *The New Yorker* and the *Atlantic,* first met Harold Ross, the *New Yorker*'s founding editor, in 1933. Morton was in the eccentric Ross' office, talking steadily about the magazine, "chattering away about what I felt to be the magazine's virtues and how various weaknesses might be shored up," he later recalled. Noticing Ross eyeing him intently, he paused:

"Goddam it," Ross said. "Let *me* talk."

What, then, does the modern American magazine amount to? Is it a civilizing force or a prescriber of soporifics? By the evidence, segments of it are one or the other to varying degrees. And some have both elements. Again it must be realized, as the housewife panelist insisted, that magazines are too unlike to be lumped. In general they may fall into classes in which function is common. Large circulation periodicals, by the costliness of simply being big, are absorbed in acting like commercial devices to keep the populace receptive to advertisers' appeals. To selected smaller magazines is left the task of fighting to keep freedom of expression unrestricted and to act as a civilizing force. Perhaps it must continue to be that we never can expect a giant magazine, heavily dependent upon its advertisers, to dedicate itself to major social change which would destroy that advertiser-publisher relationship without a substitute that will assure continued publication at the same or a better profit level.

The effect upon the public of an advertising-dependent press has been examined at length for years, particularly in the newspaper and broadcasting businesses, with magazines included at least by implication. But the magazines' part in defending freedom of the press is an untold story, largely because it has had so minor a part by comparison with newspapers and books. Not even in crisis periods, such as the days of the suits brought by the federal government against *Esquire, The American Mercury* and *Playboy* have magazines really combined to resist the censors. The few strong editorials that appeared are to be found mainly in what is dubbed the liberal magazine press, the weeklies and monthlies of public affairs and in some large daily newspapers.

The arrest and imprisonment of Ralph Ginsburg, editor and publisher of numerous magazines (*Eros, Avant-Garde* and *Fact* were among the better known), a newsletter and a few books, on untenable grounds was protested but little by other magazines. That neglect was partly, according to an analysis of the case by Merle Miller in the *New York Times Magazine,* because Ginsburg was disliked personally by many associates in journalism and book publishing. And it also was partly, as Miller does not note, because the large magazines in particular are published so far ahead of schedule that timely editorials are difficult to print effectively, although Ginsburg's case was in litigation for several years before he was imprisoned. Another explanation might be that there has been some doubt whether Ginsburg was defending his right to print sex materials or protesting because he was not allowed to make money out of his publications, all of which were marked by vulgarity.

Yet the magazines of today have an opportunity to contribute to freedom of the mind equalled only by their opportunities before and during the American Revolution and the Civil War. Freedom from a despotic foreign ruler no longer is a problem; freedom of the Afro-Americans from human slavery was won more than a century ago. But other battles for freedom are being waged: from racial and religious discrimination in all its many manifestations; from arbitrary executive decisions affecting the very lives of the people through wars fought on distant continents; from needless destruction of natural resources; from the excesses of bureaucracy; from the evils of crime; from the ruination of the cities by crowding, garbage accumulation, and industrial and vehicle pollution.

A visitor from some other planet, informed of man's plight on the American continent alone, would logically expect the citizenry, the media, the governments, the church, the schools and all other institutions to cry out incessantly for solution to these burdensome problems. Some elements of society do just that, but they are a minority: some, but by no means all, church bodies; certain segments of government; and various organizations of people of good will. A few magazines look squarely at some of these problems, to be sure, but as one looks over any news kiosk what stands forth from magazines is largely indifference to human plight (unless it be some minor personal difficulty). The scene is being changed, as already noted, but whether it is in response to faddism is not yet clear.

Where are the silent magazines at fault? Should we expect their editors to sweep out all present copy and replace it with doomsday articles about the dangers of pollution, the evils of regimes that spend billions upon deadly wars, and the greed of businessmen who strip the soil for coal or ruin the countryside with cheap buildings or unneeded bridges and highways?

To transform magazines into crusading journals overnight would lose them their readers after a few issues. They would receive letters like that sent to an abrasive "city" magazine that had began life as a combination guide-and-feature publication but later became concerned over local problems, offering only stories about anti-social actions in the city. The letter read:

> I enjoyed your magazine at first; but the character has changed so markedly that I am not renewing my subscription. What happened to those fun reviews of eating and of others of interest . . . ?

The editors and publishers must learn ways to approach such social problems deftly, to sound out the public to see how much concern there is about them, to know when the saturation point has been touched along one line or the other. That method is slow and Fabian but any other, certainly with regard to the mass appeal or general magazine, may be suicide. Yet solving that problem is part of the editor's job.

Not excused from stronger manifestations of social conscience, however, are the magazines catering to the already- or nearly-persuaded who behave as if problems do not exist for our society. Does it not behoove sailing and boating fans to be concerned with the pollution of lakes and rivers upon which their vessels float, for instance? Should the crop of new periodicals for snowmobilers not be concerned about the effects of these vehicles upon the terrain they traverse and upon the people who operate them or may be endangered by them?

Much responsibility rests upon the people who run magazines. A look at some of them is the logical next subject.

8

The
People Behind Magazines

AN INSTITUTION, Emerson said, is the lengthened shadow of one man. A magazine is such a shadow, too, although were he alive today the philosopher and magazine publisher (*The Dial*) might have changed it to "one man or one woman."

In Emerson's day the statement was more widely true than it is now. It was accurate until about the 1940's. Like the magazines, the people behind them also have been changing. The 19th century and the first half of this one produced outstanding magazines that were the shadows of editors such as William Dean Howells, Bliss Perry, H. L. Mencken, George Jean Nathan, Harold Ross, Suzanne La Follette, O. G. Villard, George Horace Lorimer, Henry R. Luce, Freda Kirchwey and various others. Today it would be difficult to assemble as lustrous a gallery, although there are some small signs that new strong editors are coming along.

In a time when readers are more often than ever before challenging what is in magazines by asking "Who says?" they want to know something about the people shaping magazines, often to their own images. This desire was dramatically demonstrated when, in 1971, Norman Cousins resigned as editor of *Saturday Review* because he disagreed with certain operating policies of the new owners and went on to establish *World*. He received impressive support at once from his *Saturday Review* readers. And the new owners of *SR* took the pains to identify themselves and their higher staff members in an attempt to continue the personal relationship of editor-to-reader that Cousins had developed over the years.

People big and little are behind magazines, although most of them are unknown to the public even in this day of personality exploitation. Here, however, we are concerned with the strong people, those with distinct concepts of what they wish to do as editors and publishers, and do it with statesmanlike ability. The people whose names live on survived, for the most part, because they contributed outstandingly to the commonweal or at least significantly to the development of the magazine as a communications medium. A test question one might put to a candidate for a magazine ownership or editorship is a quixotic and high-sounding one, perhaps, but pertinent: Has he been concerned about the survival of mankind? For, if he is indifferent to the problems inherent in that phrase, the hope that magazines will discharge their social obligations more vigorously than they do now may be in vain. Abstract, idealistic and concerned with the higher moralities as the phrase is, the total question seems far removed from the everyday tasks of planning future issues, deciding whether to shift to computerized circulation fulfillment methods or choosing the coating to use on paper. Usually such a question is left to the professional pundits, the professorial gentry with time to ponder such cosmic problems as it arouses. Yet it is relevant to the decision-making of the people behind magazines because, day after day, they will make their ultimate decisions with respect to a long-term, on-going principle.

Pointing to the people behind today's magazines, those who determine policy, is not as simple as it was half a century or more ago, when there were such strong editors as Lorimer of the *Post* and Mencken of the *Mercury*. Magazine editing and publishing were less complex in Emerson's than in Mencken's time, and are now at their most complex. Even in the early days of this century, magazine work was less of a business enterprise for the popular books because industrialization and the advertising profession were not so advanced. Certainly it was more than pure business for magazines aimed at intellectuals. Mencken, for instance, was deeply interested in literary trends and in giving promising writers sympathetic hearings. He wanted also to challenge what he considered some of the idiocies in American life—hypocrisy among the preachers, dishonesty among the businessmen and phonies among the artists. Had money-making been his or Alfred A. Knopf's prime objective, Mencken never would have edited and publisher Knopf never have supported the abrasive *American Mercury*.

The difficulty in discerning who the strong editors and publishers are these days comes about because so much is done behind the scenes. Henry Luce was a strong editor, to be sure, but after a time he removed himself from the everyday operations, for Time Inc. is far too large an operation for one person to oversee in detail. Many decisions had to be delegated. A reader wishing to identify "the brains" in the Time organization would need to check into its history at various stages, for strong personalities have been connected with its several publications and the other activities

I should think the executive editor of an electronics magazine could fix his own television!

Courtesy of *Industrial Marketing* Magazine. Cartoon by Sid Hix.

of this communications empire. With such big enterprises it is practical only to portray someone typical of those who exert considerable internal influence.

Reports on active top executives are all well and good. But what of the hard-working, self-effacing persons who actually are more powerful in setting policy or establishing tone and attitude than their employers may suspect? They are difficult to identify and rarely publicized. The author remembers the instance of a large specialized firm of magazine publishers in the middle west with which he was connected for a time. The real publishing genius was the owner's secretary. Her organizing skill and judgment were acknowledged and recognized generally although in those days, long before women were more given to asserting their rights than they have been since, some of the career-bent men with bigger salaries and grand titles resented her. On the owner-publisher's death she became the new company president in his place. Everyone realized, even if grudgingly, that she knew more about the business than any other person. She ran the firm for a number of years thereafter, and just as successfully. It is a common experience, as well, for the editor or publisher of a magazine that has won an award to single out one or two persons who really have shaped its formula and format and to insist that they be given the credit.

Discovering the impress of an individual on a magazine is fascinating activity, something like possessing expertise in graphology. Just as writers usually reveal their personalities through their styles (Ernest Hemingway, the professional he-man, for example, wrote with the brutal terseness he affected in his life-style and selected his subject matter to match). Similarly, magazine proprietors and editors reveal themselves. *Physical Culture,* an extraordinarily popular magazine once put out by Bernarr Macfadden, echoed his eccentricities and philosophy (like his belief in food faddism and certain exercises) and it may be recalled that he still was parachuting from planes while in his 80's. *Vogue* was Edna Woolman Chase, *Harper's Bazaar* was Carmel Snow, *Ballyhoo* was Norman Anthony, Edward Weeks was the *Atlantic,* Frederick Lewis Allen had been *Harper's,* and so on into dozens of examples from recent magazine history.

Ben Hibbs, one of the noted editors of *The Saturday Evening Post,* is a middle-of-the-roader politically and socially, making no pretensions at artiness or sophistication; the *Post* in his day reflected his commonsensical and conservative view. On the other hand, Frank Crowinshield, editor of *Vanity Fair,* now indistinguishably incorporated into *Vogue,* was an aesthete, a word-taster, somewhat flamboyant, witty and playful. He made his magazine clever, satirical and captious—just like himself.

Unquestionably, the largest magazine in the history of publishing, in terms of number of copies sold, *Reader's Digest* is in the image of its founders, who have had an extraordinary ability to gauge the interests of the middle class of any country where they publish. Of this husband-and-wife team, Mr. and Mrs. DeWitt Wallace, we shall hear more later in the chapter.

Readers are not always aware of the unseen influences working on the periodicals they read. And executives are important influences. How many subscribers ever have seen, much less talked with, an officer of a popular magazine? Television acquaintance, if any, is the usual limit. Some millions of persons are aware of William F. Buckley, Jr., editor and publisher of the *National Review,* a small, conservative opinion bi-weekly, because of his television program "Firing Line," but it is not exactly regarded as a popular publication. Only now and then are other V.I.P.'s of the publishing world on the screen.

Major owners, such as the Wallaces, Walter Annenberg and Samuel I. Newhouse, often use their publications to advance their social views. They and others like them dine at the White House (or at least are invited), receive public appointments, and some government officials give their publications preferential treatment because they may be friendly to the regime in power. All this happens no matter which political party is in office. Readers should know, therefore, of the biases of the magazine owners, but be reminded at the same time that no such owner should be deprived of the right to such associations. Nor should that owner deprive his staff members of the right to their associations or refuse space to points of view in disagreement with his own.

Such a liberal policy is particularly important for consumer magazines that aim for the general public. One does not expect many-sidedness from such partisan journals as *The Nation* and the *National Review,* to name ideological opposites. But one does expect breadth and tolerance from *McCall's, Reader's Digest, The New Yorker, Time* and other magazines intended for a substantial audience.

De Witt and Lila Acheson Wallace

Examining the lives of a few strong editors and owners of present-day magazines will suffice to show the types of persons who control or have much to say about a number of important magazines in America—types that represent scores of other persons who have not made it so big but follow similar philosophies, whatever they may be, on a smaller scale.

A. Kent MacDougall, for some years the *Wall Street Journal's* press specialist and one of the few published media evaluators, once told a story about the *Digest,* whose co-owners are the first to be dealt with in this chapter. The joke, he said, was going the rounds of publishing circles. It concerned a writer who produced the perfect *Digest* article. "Originally," MacDougall wrote, "he wrote it as a how-to-do-it piece; the *Digest* successively urged him to transform it into a personal-experience story, and to inject notes of spiritual uplift and of concern over the menace of communism. It emerged entitled: 'How I Fought a Grizzly Bear for the FBI and Found God.' "

Such tales stem for the image of themselves DeWitt and Lila Wallace have cast through their enormously successful magazine. For they have imparted their social view unfailingly over the years of control, which now exceed 50. The idea for the publication occurred to Wallace while he was recuperating in a French hospital after World War I. He had been hit by shrapnel in the Meuse-Argonne offensive in 1918. James Playsted Wood, historian of the *Digest,* reports that "Wallace found that he could satisfactorily condense articles of what he considered lasting interest from the current magazines." He envisioned a small monthly made up of such material. That was in 1919. After six months he submitted sample copies to the leading magazine publishing firms.

"The publishers could not have cared less," Wood relates. The only encouragement came from William R. Hearst, who said *Reader's Digest* might reach 300,000 circulation. Wallace was thoroughly discouraged and nearly abandoned the entire plan. But in 1921 the support of his newly acquired wife, Lila Acheson, and the enthusiasm of a fellow worker at Westinghouse decided him to try his magazine on his own. The "little wonder," as John Bainbridge called it years later in a *New Yorker* article, went on to fabulous success.

Until 1955 the magazine refused advertising. At first, also, it depended upon already-printed material for its source of editorial copy. The latter policy was changed to one of accepting some original manuscripts and placing them in certain other magazines before digesting. Then they were published in both.

Wallace, tall and shy, and Mrs. Wallace, petite, artistic and less retiring than her husband, from the first set the social philosophy of their magazine. It scarcely has varied since, although new fields have been added to receive the same conservative treatment.

The first issue, dated February 1922, bore such article titles as: "How to Keep Young Mentally." "Love—Luxury or Necessity?" "Whatever is New for Women is Wrong." "Progress in Science."

During its entire life thus far, the amazing magazine—amazing because of its world circulation of nearly 30-million, its 30 different editions in 14 languages, its educational edition, its condensed books, and its records—has consistently followed a set of policies laid down by the Wallaces. Among these are opposition to what it considers un-Americanism, support of a strong military establishment, severe criticism of communist nations, and objections to welfare state practices. Such views are not expressed in any direct editorial statement, for the magazine does not print editorials. The *Digest* has been condemned and praised fiercely. Its giant readership, which may be 150 million persons monthly, must be a strong influence in the creation of middle American opinion.

Although the Wallaces spend less time in the magazine's direction than they used to, it still gives off the aura of its early days, which has been described as that of the old fashioned Sunday school. If that is so, it is not surprising, since DeWitt Wallace's father was a Presbyterian pastor and his mother the child of another minister. The optimistic philosophy of the magazine comes from Wallace's evangelistic zeal. Often the viewpoint permits avoidance of certain unpleasant topics and of taking a hard, socially-critical stance.

Some years ago the author had occasion to ask the Wallaces about their personal interests. A telegraphed reply observed that *"The Digest* includes such wide array of subjects we have felt no need for outside interests or hobbies. We have believed concentration on magazine more important and far more challenging." This statement says a good deal about the couple. But it is modest, for each has been generous in philanthropy, aiding education and the opera world with large gifts.

One other Wallace policy must be mentioned: the company's generosity as well to its writers. The author was present when a free-lance writer friend received an unasked-for letter from DeWitt Wallace containing a check for $1,500, with the explanation that his articles always had been welcome and that here was further appreciation. Yet the writer never had seen Wallace. Payment of large sums even when rejecting a manuscript, if the writer had been encouraged to go ahead, has for years been a set policy. And the fees for articles and payments of expenses are higher than those of almost all other U.S. magazines.

NORMAN COUSINS

In philosophical contrast to the Wallaces is the background of Norman Cousins, editor of *World,* which was founded in 1972, but for 30 years identified with *Saturday Review,* from which he had resigned the year before.

Twice the New York *Times* has featured Cousins as its "Man in the News" and once devoted a special article to him. The first time, in 1966, it headed the piece "Watchful Citizen." The second, in 1971, was titled "Unyielding Editor." In 1972 it punned with "A New World for Norman Cousins." The same year another publication, *Journalism Quarterly,* reported on a study of Cousins' views and put this headline on it: "N.C.: Editor as Persuader." A few months later the Cleveland *Press* ran a syndicated article in which it also used a pun by labelling it "Cousins has New World to Conquer."

These four headings summarize well the type of person who is N.C., the initials which have appeared for so many years at the ends of his editorials. A new reader of any magazine with which Cousins may be connected would, from these titles alone, know what to expect—for Cousins indeed has long been a watchful, unyielding and evangelistic magazine editor, but from a far different point of view than the Wallaces'.

Although Cousins in some ways is an exceptional magazine journalist he is not an odd type, for he has counterparts on some of the opinion magazines and among the little magazines of literature and public affairs. But in one way he is extraordinary, for his type rarely is found at the helm of an influential periodical of a major publishing firm more given to issuing large, money-making books than "idea" periodicals. The company that gave him and his magazine shelter, and a free rein, was for some years the McCall Corp. *Saturday Review* was financially successful under Cousins' guidance but, nevertheless, McCall did not interfere while Cousins did as he wished in espousing humanitarian causes, some running counter to certain conventional political and social opinions. Nor did it try to persuade him to go after a monster circulation, approximating the many millions of its *McCall's* and *Redbook* magazines. *Saturday Review* was, as it still is under its present ownership, an unusual combination of financial success and capability of appeal to people interested in ideas and social change.

Cousins is unlike the Wallaces in philosophy and in method. Each is respected, even if not agreed with, because a position is taken. At least readers know where these editors stand. Otherwise, however, there is little in common.

Journalism, in Cousins' view, must have a larger purpose than making money—which does not even come first, for he believes competent publications will not suffer from high quality, although they never may reach a mass circulation—yet he had brought the *Review* to 660,000 a week when he left it. He told Ralph Novak, writing for the Newspaper Enterprise Association in 1972, that he sees two ways to edit a magazine. "You can get a marketing organization to tell you what people want and then edit to meet their needs," he said. "Or you can edit to please yourself, as I do, and hope that enough people share your enthusiasm and concerns to make the magazine a success."

And he does not see his magazine, as the Wallaces see theirs, as a conveyor belt to advance the conservative viewpoint of resisting active social change. To please Cousins it must transmit ideas and facts that will help persuade or evangelize readers to the opposite view—that there must be social change if man is to live in a sane world.

Little has been revealed about Cousins that would explain his outlook, which Paul E. Nelson, in the *Journalism Quarterly* article, considered that of a secular evangelist preaching in the interest of United World Federalists with its goals of world law and government and other ideals. As yet there has been no published biography and Cousins has said little about himself in any of his own books, including *Present Tense,* which contains a long chapter on the *Saturday Review* and many editorials from the magazine while it was under his tenure.

The few biographical details help by inference. Born in 1915 in Union Hill, New Jersey, Cousins, according to what relatives once told the New York *Times,* was a frail and serious boy, so serious he was called "The Professor" even when he was five, if an uncle is to be believed. When he was 11 he was placed in a sanitorium because tuberculosis was suspected, but fortunately proved to be unfounded. This experience, he said years later, led him to have "a new respect for the preciousness of life." That realization may be at the base of his many humanitarian interests and activities. In 1964, when he was almost 50, he again was ill, becoming partly paralyzed. The condition ceased unexplainably.

His youth was spent in New York City, where he attended Teachers College, Columbia University. Cousins' journalistic life began in 1935, as education editor of the New York *Post;* his first magazine job followed when he became literary and managing editor of *Current History.* From there he moved to *Saturday Review,* which then had *of Literature* as part of its title. That was in 1940. He changed the 20-year-old magazine from a purely literary one, struggling to survive, to one dealing with public affairs as well. Circulation rose steadily from the 30,000 it had when he took over.

But late in 1971, after 31 years with the magazine, he resigned. The McCall Book Co., its then owner, had sold it to Saturday Review Industries that July. Soon Cousins disagreed with the new owners' plans to change the format and formula, sell each week's issue separately from the rest (thus creating four periodicals, each on a different main topic, like science and the arts), launch a book club and a book publishing division. Henry Raymont, reporting the editor's decision in the New York *Times,* said that what led to the resignation seemed to amount to a combination of clashing philosophical outlooks, conflicts with young men over display and promotion, and discrepancies between editorial and business concepts.

"I object strongly to the commercial use of the *Saturday Review* subscription list for purposes that have nothing to do with the magazine," Cousins said. "I object to the exploitation of the name of the *Review* for sundry marketing ventures. That name may no longer belong to the people who created it, but the people who created it have a duty to make known their concern."

Such a view was to be expected from someone who had identified himself with numerous causes: co-chairman of the National Committee for a Sane Nuclear Policy, honorary president of United World Federalists, and orginator of the "Hiroshima Maidens" program to aid victims of the atomic bombing. These are only several of many activities. Cousins also is author or editor of books about Jawaharlal Nehru and Albert Schweitzer. He is a first-class photographer as well.

The appearance of the "World" in two of the stories about Cousins are references both to his new magazine and the difficulties he faced starting it. From the early issues of *World: A Review of Ideas, Creative Arts and the Human Condition* it was obvious that there had been no compromise with the high ideals presented in *Saturday Review* in his day. But whether the new magazine would survive was yet to be tested at this writing.

A reader aware of the background of Norman Cousins will know what to expect. He will be repelled or attracted, depending upon his point of view. But if a Cousins' personality, even though enlightening a reader about the journalism involved, exerts no pull because of its unswervingly lofty tone, there are numerous alternatives. One such is Hugh M. Hefner, founder, owner and editor of *Playboy* and of several other magazines, and head of numerous non-publishing ventures.

Hugh M. Hefner

The public mind for years has had a picture of magazines as colorful printed pieces existing to make money and to help people pass the time. In these days such time-killing takes place when the television set is "kaput" or when a reader is stuck in a long wait at a doctor's office, barber shop or bus terminal. That situation is changing, however, as the public becomes better educated and demands more of magazines than entertainment.

Hundreds of periodicals are still being published on the assumption that entertaining the reader is no sin and is a perfectly legitimate function as journalism—as, of course, it is. Consequently, there are the few that purvey humor and satire, the many fan magazines devoted to people and events in the worlds of sport, television, radio, cinema, stage and other entertainment areas, and a long shelf which supports more or less similar magazines offering articles, stories and cartoons that depend upon sex to gain and hold readers. Usually the subjects are treated hedonistically.

The magazine that leads the entertainment group comes from this last category. Its owner-publisher has become the symbol of hedonism in magazine journalism. The combination, of course, is *Playboy* and Hugh Marston Hefner. This duo has been taken seriously enough to be the subject of three books, one a serious examination of what is known as the Playboy Philosophy, which is a long series of articles by Hefner explaining his viewpoint on censorship and other topics. No one as yet, however, has told the full story of the publisher's life, but some future biographer will find a treasure in scrapbooks Hefner has been compiling on himself —by the late 1960's, it has been reported, these had reached more than 80 volumes.

Few magazine readers need briefing on *Playboy,* for it has been well-publicized and its name used in many other connections, chiefly the companion enterprises of the conglomerate of which it is a part. As a reader, one should note how it avoids subtlety, gratifies interest in illustrations of nudes (almost always female), offers sexy books and cartoons, short stories and jokes usually relying on sex for their point, and fills the interstices largely with short articles on sex or important present-day issues, often by "name" writers, including some of the keenest thinkers around.

As an example of a magazine that is a mirror reflection of its owner, *Playboy* is perfect. For it portrays the life and interests of Hefner as surely as *Saturday Review* for many years did the life and interests of Norman Cousins, and *Reader's Digest* those of the Wallaces. Perhaps that is why the history of *Playboy* (*Big Bunny,* by Joe Goldberg) is sufficiently biographical, skimpy as the life-story portion turns out to be. There may be

Cartoon by Edmund C. Arnold.

nothing more to Hugh Hefner than Playboy Enterprises, for people are
known by their works, it is said. His works include building a magazine
which, between 1953 and 1973 has climbed to more than seven-million
circulation with abundant advertising in every issue, a series of night
clubs, resorts and hotels, other publications, and such lesser works as
Playboy cufflinks, ties, books and calendars. Hefner, perhaps, is equated
with a symbol—that of the bunny, a striking young woman, occasionally
not Caucasian, with rabbit ears at the back of her head and dressed so as
to show off her sex characteristics. An ornament of the Playboy clubs,
the rabbit symbol does not end there. It also is to be found on casino doors,
movie theatres, a film division, greeting cards, music and records, a model
agency, beer mugs, earrings, parkas, key chains and tie clips.

What was the development of this fantastically successful financial career for Hefner? He began life in Chicago in 1926. After being in the U.S. Army from 1944 to 1946 he went to the University of Illinois, getting a bachelor's degree with a major in psychology three years later. He tried free-lance advertising copy writing, then wrote circulation promotion pieces for *Esquire* in Chicago in 1951. One of his next two jobs had an ironical twist on the face of it. He was promotion manager for Publishers Development Corp. in 1952 and the next year circulation manager of *Children's Activities,* a useful and innocent enough periodical issued by a firm also engaged in publishing girlie magazines.

The usual story about Hefner's launching of *Playboy* in 1953 is that, while he was an *Esquire* employee at $60 a week, the firm decided to move its magazines to New York. It gave employees raises if they would move. Hefner was offered, the account goes, a $20 increase, but insisted on $25. He was refused and quit. Arnold Gingrich, now publisher of *Esquire* but in Hefner's day there the magazine's chief editor, denies this account, however. The truth was, he wrote in his memoirs, that Hefner refused to move although that would have brought him a cost of living salary increase.

In any case, Hefner started *Playboy* in competition with *Esquire,* but was not sanguine of its success, since he did not even date the first issue. He need not have worried. The magazine now has its own tall building in Chicago. In the meantime he married, was divorced after five years, and has two children.

His multi-millionaire's life has corresponded at many points with the image of the ideal man as created by the magazine. Those persons who have described his habits provide ample detail. His parties are famous. His travels in his private jet, his huge circular bed on which he often does editorial work, his liking for pajamas and lounging robes instead of suits while working, and his retinue of business or other attendants in his Chicago mansion all are part of the *Playboy* image—a fantasy come true.

Perhaps almost as revealing of him as his sybaritic life is the attenuated essay called the "Playboy Philosophy" which began in the December 1962 issue and ran for two years, totaling 25 installments. Essentially a defense of *Playboy's* formula, it became, for the more thoughtful readers, the rationale for living a life of pleasure, of doing what one pleases whenever and wherever. Hefner appears to have written it himself. It is disorganized and undisciplined enough as a piece of writing to be in truth the work of a single writer who had not subjected his work to editing and also was writing, from month to month, with no two-year plan to follow, for the document grew gradually. A few highlights from it:

> If sex were the principal reason for *Playboy's* popularity, of course, then the magazine's several dozen imitators—almost all of

which are far sexier than we—would be the ones with the larger circulations.

It has long seemed quite incredible—indeed, incomprehensible— to us that detailed descriptions of murder, which we consider a crime, are acceptable in our art and literature, while detailed descriptions of sex, which is not a crime, are prohibited. It is as though our society put hate above love—favored death over life.

A concentrated interest in the affairs of others may produce some worthwhile ends, but it can also be the basis for meddlesome disruption of other people's private lives. We have always been a little suspicious of those too aggressively concerned with the welfare of their fellowmen.

The first quotation, from the Philosophy's opening installment, is perhaps typical of the depth of the series. Hefner overlooks the skill of his well-paid cartoonists, his use of copyright-free classical sex fables and the resources he has had available, except at the very beginning, to pay leading writers treating sex subjects in both fiction and non-fiction. The success of *Penthouse,* a rival imported from England early in this decade, moved Hefner to establish a new magazine, *Oui,* so he could compete with the British invader, indicating that competition can become a threat.

However, Hefner's view, that the magazine must offer more than sex content, is being justified. From him—or perhaps from his gifted, ever-loyal first commander, the late A. C. Spectorsky—came the decisions about just what to include beyond pictures of nudes. Short stories by such noted authors as Lawrence Durrell, Bernard Malamud, John Updike, Vladimir Nabokov and James Baldwin appeared. International figures were interviewed at such excessive length, sometimes, that one wonders how many readers had the staying power to reach the end. Thus the intellectual facet of Hugh Hefner gains steady representation. The magazine also has gone beyond sex content by its attention to men's fashions, useful as well as an adjunct in advertising, and to cooking possibilities for men.

PATRICIA CARBINE

Thus far men have been presented here as leading magazine figures. In this day of the women's liberation movement, however, it would seem unfitting to omit women editors or publishers although, to be sure, there have been far fewer women than men at the top posts in the magazine world, as in most other professions. Women have bossed, if rarely owned, big magazines since 1838, beginning with that fascinating lady editor, Sarah Josepha Hale, who dominated *Godey's Lady Book* for 40 years.

Numerous magazines for women as well as for other readers have had distinguished staff members since then. Putting the stamps of their personalities unforgettably on their publications were such strong editors of fairly recent years as Edna Woolman Chase, Diana Vreeland and Jessica Daves of *Vogue;* Carmel White Snow and Nancy White of *Harper's Bazaar;* Beatrice Blackmar Gould of *The Ladies' Home Journal;* and Betsy Talbot Blackwell of *Mademoiselle.* In the present decade we find Enid A. Haupt editing *Seventeen;* Helen Gurley Brown in charge at *Cosmopolitan;* Patricia Carbine running the new *Ms;* and Geraldine Rhoads leading *Woman's Day.* Before them, on periodicals not intended for women, were Clara Savage Littledale of *Parents* and Ada Campbell Rose of *Jack and Jill.* Mary Mapes Dodge was not only editor of the beloved *St. Nicholas* but also a highly successful children's novelist. And then there was the sensational Mrs. Frank Leslie, who continued her husband's various popular and specialized magazines successfully for years during the 19th century.

Patricia Carbine represents a combination of a woman's magazine journalist with first class experience on both a mass general magazine and a mass women's magazine. She abandoned both to embark on a new and somewhat speculative venture, a new type of women's magazine which may be destined for a limited circulation.

Except for her rich consumer magazine experience, her background is not extraordinary. Up to a certain point it is much like that of any American journalist of either sex. Patricia Carbine grew up in an Irish Catholic family in Philadelphia, although born in Villanova, Pa., in 1932. Her parents' parents were all Irish-born. She went to a Catholic school, Mater Misericordiae, in Merion, Pa., where she edited the yearbook, an opportunity she welcomed since she had an editing career in mind even in the seventh grade. She went on with scholastic journalism by editing the Rosemont College paper; she received her B.A. from that institution in 1952. Miss Carbine's entry into professional journalism occurred the next year at Cowles, starting as an editorial researcher on *Look.* Before she resigned from that magazine in 1969 she had been assistant editor, a senior editor, assistant and then managing editor, and finally executive editor.

Whether she saw the disaster coming at Cowles Communications, which would leave the corporation without any of its magazines in a few years, is not clear but in 1970, after 17 years with *Look,* she left it for the editorial directorship of *McCall's,* the largest, in circulation, of the group of multi-million circulation magazines in its field. By then Patricia Theresa Carbine, to use her full name, was known as one of the ablest editors in the profession, man or woman alike, but more as an administrator than as a policy-maker. Then, in early 1972, she resigned to become editor-in-chief and publisher of *Ms,* a new monthly considered the voice of the liberated woman. It has been defined by one of its founders and editors, Gloria Steinem, as a magazine for the "concerned and aware woman who knows something is happening and needs intelligent, honest information on how to deal with the changing roles of the female in American life," as she explained it to *Harper's Bazaar* in 1971.

So close a connection with the women's rights movement as the editorship of a magazine that is spokeswoman for it was not hinted in her final months at *Look*. Her views may have changed because of her *McCall's* tenure, for it certainly is a far more orthodox and conventional magazine for women than *Ms* so far has turned out to be. While at *Look,* as late as mid-1970, Miss Carbine told George J. Barmann, a Cleveland *Plain Dealer* staff writer who interviewed her, "I am not a woman's libber . . . I agree with many of their premises but I deplore the invasion of premises to make a point." (This reference was to the time when a group of women stormed into the offices of *The Ladies' Home Journal.*)

Yet she also told Barmann: "I think the worst thing you can say about a woman in business, in any business, is that she 'thinks like a man.' " She also discussed women's magazines, revealing her attitude toward them. "They have never seemed very challenging to me, I'm afraid, because I'm basically undomestic." The challenge at *Ms* apparently has been greater—and therefore more rewarding than at *McCall's.*

A reader aware that magazine publishers, consciously or unconsciously, develop a formula for a magazine can compare *McCall's* and *Ms* and decide how the Carbine temperament would find much to bore her in the older and larger magazine, which in the early 1970's had about 8 million circulation—*Ms* two years later had only around 250,000. The lack of interest in matters domestic might explain the boredom. Miss Carbine, also, at the time of the interview was single, lived in a one-bedroom mid-town apartment suite, and said she likes to travel. Only the food portion of *McCall's* standard woman's magazine content could have much interest for her.

All but she of about a dozen women at a staff meeting of *Ms* were wearing pants suits. But Mary Breasted, of *Saturday Review,* reported in an article about the magazine, that Miss Carbine as well as Miss Steinem were deferred to by all the others, despite the editor's refusal that day to be conventionally unconventional. And, the *SR* writer noted, it was Miss Carbine who stuck to practical details, like cutting down on overtime costs. It was she who explained how the magazine reaches newsstands, and admitted that it was paying newsdealers what is called "a display allowance," to be sure it is seen by the public.

Ms, however, is far more concerned about present-day social problems and ideas of interest to women than all but one or two of its competitors. Its publisher and chief editor face the problem, nevertheless, of keeping it from becoming a narrow, monotonous cause-publication dealing exclusively with woman's liberation topics. But, as Miss Carbine told the author soon after she took over, other topics will be treated, although from the viewpoint of the woman interested in a better deal for women in the professions, politics and in all other areas where they should exercise choice. This difficult matter of formula is on top of all the usual ones of securing enough advertising accounts and readers to stay in business and somehow contending with mounting operating costs.

In answer to Miss Breasted's question, what will *Ms* do if the women's movement fizzles, Miss Carbine said: "Once the ideas that the movement does embody are truly accepted, society is going to have to work out whole new ways of dealing with our lives, with the world. If we are truly on the threshold of a new phase of human development, I think it's reasonable to assume that a medium reporting on and reflecting that development has to be in business for a long, long time."

JOHN H. JOHNSON

One other minority group has had a more or less unrecognized part in American magazine journalism but now is gaining recognition. It is the black journalists engaged in publishing and editing magazines for their fellows. Few whites—and even many black readers—are aware of the extent of the black magazine business or of some of the outstanding writers, editors and publishers coming from that group over the years. W. E. B. Du Bois, for instance, was a late 19th and early 20th century sociologist and writer who founded and edited five magazines, of which two are still published: *The Crisis* and *Phylon.* Today there are such important publishers and editors as W. Leonard Evans, who issues *Tuesday* and *Tuesday-at-Home,* and John H. Johnson, who heads a firm producing four magazines, including *Ebony* and *Jet.* Three of these last four named are in the million or more circulation list.

Non-black readers aware of the black magazine enterprises usually know of John H. Johnson, or at least of *Ebony,* the flagship of his magazine publishing empire. And an empire it is, for it consists not only of the *Life*-like monthly but also of *Black World,* devoted each month to the literary, artistic and to some extent the political aspects of the black society in America; *Jet,* a weekly newsmagazine of about a half-million circulation; and *Black Stars,* a fan magazine feeding the insatiable interest Americans of all racial origins have in figures of the entertainment world— in this instance, the financially successful popular black singers, actors and comedians. Johnson also publishes a line of books, conducts a book club and heads or is active in various other types of businesses, including an insurance firm and a manufacturer of cosmetics. He has become a millionaire in the process. In 1972, his then 30-year-old Johnson Publishing Co. opened a new 11-story building in downtown Chicago. It is as luxurious as any giant, white-owned publishing firm.

Thus far John Johnson may appear to be simply a DeWitt Wallace of another race. In certain respects he is. He has built a huge organization, has become personally wealthy, supports essentially cautious and, in the past at least, even reactionary social forces, and has endowed most of his magazines with his personal social philosophy. The resemblance has led some members of his own race to condemn him as an Uncle Tom. But in two vital respects he is not a black Wallace. First, he publishes one magazine which is so different from his others and so involved in encouraging a point of view counter to that found during most of their years of publication of all his other magazines that one wonders why he countenances it. This rebel is *Black World,* his first magazine and for most of its life thus far called *Negro Digest,* and originally much like *Reader's Digest.* Under an argumentative, unrelenting, white-hating editor named Hoyt Fuller in recent years it has been filled with revolutionary ardor. The further test of Johnson's tolerance of dissent within his own publishing family is that this particular magazine is a steady loser. His counterparts in the white publishing world may carry a profitless magazine for a time but then kill it; and certainly there would be no tolerance of one that runs philosophically counter to much that the owner appears to believe in.

A second difference, which may go a little distance to explain the first but only in most recent years, is that Johnson's views on social matters are changing. Not that he ever was indifferent to the needs of the black society in America. But his concept of that society's needs is altering, as is what he can do about it. Until about the mid-1960's, he was content to hold before his readers the Horatio Alger ideal of accumulating money and property and of living in ultimate comfort, even ostentatious display, not particularly in his own life but in the lives of others. He used to play up the stories of black millionaires. Personal financial success was emphasized but the need for social change, for a better deal for all black people, was subordinated.

But as the civil rights movement gained momentum and then the militants made themselves heard, Johnson's perspectives swerved somewhat. The change is reflected in his magazines' pages. He is no revolutionary warrior, violent or non-violent, by any way you measure him. However, he has come to understand that the black *bourgeoisie* is not the core of the black society in America. And he is tolerant of ideas to a measure and risk to himself that few major publishers can equal. Such a change does not come easily. Fuller, *Black World's* editor, complained in an interview with *Black Collegian* magazine that the publishing company gives his magazine "virtually no promotion." Johnson, he said, resisted changing the

name from *Negro Digest* to *Black World* but finally acceded, probably because the *Digest* was his first publication, but also because it seemed to be
leaning toward militancy. The main fact, however, is that Johnson has allowed the magazine to go on. Perhaps he can write off the losses, but his
relationship to the excitable, fire-eating contributors is there to see.

The source of Johnson's interest in basic civil rights for black people
is no different than that of most persons of his race—he began poor. He
and his mother had gone to Chicago from rural Arkansas, where he was
born in 1917, to visit the Chicago World's Fair of 1933. His father died
when John was six. They decided to stay in the north, living on relief. He
went to high school, where an insurance company president heard his
honors convocation speech, liked it, and encouraged Johnson to go to
college. He gave the future publisher a part-time job; meantime Johnson
took classes at the University of Chicago.

Asked to work on the company's house magazine, he got from this
experience not only a liking for journalism but also the idea that other
black citizens would appreciate a publication consisting of articles about
the black society. He mortgaged his mother's furniture for $500 and
launched *Negro Digest*. That was 1942. Three years later *Ebony* was born,
offering an optimistic view of black life in America, emphasizing success
but saying relatively little about the worst of the injustices and inequities
in work opportunities, education, housing, the arts and virtually all other
aspects of life for black people. There followed various other periodicals
and related enterprises, not all of which succeeded. After *Ebony* came
Jet, Tan Confessions, Hue, Copper Romance and *Ebony International*.
The last three were discontinued, *Tan Confessions* became *Tan* and then
Black Stars.

In the early 1970's *Ebony* has 1,300,000 circulation each month
and is lush with advertising of high quality. *Jet* has nearly half-a-million
a week but with relatively little advertising, although it is increasing in
volume. *Black World* sells almost no external advertising space and Johnson does not reveal its circulation. By the nature of its content it must be
around 30,000. *Black Stars* already has captured substantial sales in the
new formula but its circulation had not settled down at this writing. And
then there is the new building on Michigan Avenue.

The black readers of these Johnson publications have a predictable
reaction to them and to their ebullient and hearty owner, proud of his ac-
complishments and of his organization. The older middle class, a growing
body as conditions are improved even so slightly as they have been for
this minority group, enjoy *Ebony* and respect Johnson as a success they
wish they could emulate. The younger middle class responds to *Black
Stars*. The busy, news-hungry, mostly professionals and inside workers,
read *Jet*. The militant and literary-artistic readers ignore these three as

irrelevant and Uncle Tomish, as part of the Establishment and not to be trusted. Some cleave to *Black World,* especially if they are in the clique supporting it. None of these magazines, not even the latter, portrays fully the lives and interests of the bulk of the American black population but neither, for that matter, does any other. Perhaps to see more of the whole racial scene a reader must read these and also certain quasi-magazines like *Muhammad Speaks* and *The Black Panther* for a broader view, although both are distorted by the propagandas of their sponsors, the Nation of Islam and the Black Panther Party.

Do any of these editors and publishers and their enterprises, whatever their race or color, actually have influence? Undoubtedly most believe they are influential. If they are, how significant is that power?

9

Power and Influence

Scanlan's, a muckraking magazine that lasted a few years until the early 1970's, once ran an article called "Dirty Kitchens of New York," that exposed certain restaurant conditions. Shortly thereafter the Health Service Administration formed a special investigating team and announced that it now would make public the names of the offending places. A long list of such establishments appeared in New York newspapers. As time went on, identification of places that had improved their kitchens was printed as well. The practice has continued ever since.

This example, typical of a kind common during the past century, is one evidence of power exercised by magazines as well as other media that has been exerted in various areas of our social life. President William Howard Taft, in 1912, established a Commission of Industrial Relations that had been suggested two months earlier by participants in a symposium run by *Survey* magazine discussing the bombing case of the McNamara brothers. John McNamara was a union official involved in a disagreement with California industrial interests. Professor John H. Schacht of the University of Illinois College of Communications, in his study of opinion magazines, cited that example and various others to indicate magazine influence. There also was the *National Review's* "significant part" in the nomination of Senator Barry Goldwater as candidate for the presidency in 1964. Other instances can be spotted in the histories of *Commentary, The Reporter, Commonweal* and scores more from the days early in the century when *Collier's, Everybody's* and other influential periodicals were thriving and from later when the original *Saturday Evening Post* was alive.

The classic example of magazine impact, however, is the aftermath of a 1935 article by J. C. Furnas in *Reader's Digest,* "—And Sudden Death." Shockingly realistic, it was a piece about the need to curb automobile highway accidents, giving bloody details of calamities resulting from careless and reckless driving. It became what may be so far the most widely-read article in magazine history. James Playsted Wood, in his history of the *Digest,* points out that it was subsequently syndicated as a comic strip, made into a movie, and within three months after publication some four million reprints had been requested. It was discussed at thousands of club meetings. Copies were put in packages with new auto license plates. Wood records another chapterful of effective articles from the *Digest* over the years. And he reports still more historical examples from other periodicals in another of his books, citing magazine contents which led to election of a governor and support for a mountain school, for instance.

Wood also notes that indirect or secondary influence exists as well, in sermons, speeches and books inspired by magazine content. To that can be added the fact that the American language has been affected by magazines—both fiction and non-fiction have carried regional English, as well as experimental writing, throughout the nation. Widely used in classrooms are numerous magazines special-educational editions, which have stimulated interest in language and creative writing through competitions. Influence is exerted by the magazine's editorial function of offering readers ideas and information not commonly found in other media—such as poetry, plays, novels, short stories. New trends and applications of art, design and photography appear in magazines as well. Many periodicals featuring fashions, home furnishings, food, housekeeping, hobbies, sports, architecture and other interests have had an influence upon people's dress, eating habits, and leisure-time use.

The nature and value of these influences are not being argued nor is their impartiality defended. What is being observed is that such influence exists—considering the billions of copies of magazines issued annually in the U.S.A. alone.

INFLUENCE OF THE WOMEN'S MAGAZINES

For years, leading magazines aimed at women have had long-range effects in creating stereotypes in their readers' minds. The American female, from young girlhood on, has been encouraged by these periodicals to believe in certain circumstances as normal and to be taken for granted—for example, that the primary goal is to be taken care of by a man, preferably through marriage. In any case, to achieve the goal in one manner or the other it is necessary to be physically as attractive as possible. So she has been taught by them that the intellectual woman will offend certain types of men and really attract few; that a multitude of pastes, salves and fluids is essential to survival as well as beauty; that clothing and jewelry of certain types are inseparable from social success; that consideration of one's personal success is one of the most important activities of womankind, perhaps second, only to husband and children (if there are any).

For the most part, women have been portrayed by magazines as not really interested in public affairs, certainly not to the exclusion of what touched their lives more personally. Until recent years, when enough women clamored for broader content than the health, fashion, cooking and gardening material—which still dominates some of the glossy periodicals—there was little discussion of political and economic problems. Racial injustice was scarcely mentioned—on the contrary, a black reader of the women's magazines would only rarely find a black face looking out at her from their pages unless it be an occasional picture of a Marian Anderson, a Leontyne Price or some other non-white of indisputable accomplishment. Editors of mass magazines gave major attention to whites because the others "did not count."

Not that readers of women's magazines are without information from other sources on the vital subjects affecting the whole of society. Newspapers, other magazines more specialized or broader of mind, at least portions of television and radio time, even certain motion pictures, fill the gaps. From them is obtained material about what is happening to the environment, attempted governmental restraints on the media, and abuse of the consumer by some manufacturers of products women buy for those bodies and homes their own magazines usually put foremost issue after issue. But not until consumerism became an increasingly powerful force have women's magazines faced such subjects head on. When women, acknowledged as our chief consumers, became concerned, consumerism was in.

THE EDITORIAL-ADVERTISING SYNDROME

More subtle is the influence of the "cooperation" between the editorial and advertising departments evident in several of the major magazines for women. This includes such mention of advertisers' products in editorial content and then only those of particular advertisers, a practice easily verified by looking at issues of *Vogue, Harper's Bazaar, Essence* or *Glamour,* for example. Articles protesting these relationships have been published for years, usually in a tone of shocked surprise that such practices are condoned. But the policy of cooperation is so ingrained and taken for granted in the publishing business generally that objectors to it are considered extremists or radicals.

Despite this commonality, the playing of mutually helpful games by publishers and the advertisers who keep commercial magazines alive has its impact. A magazine that prints cover pictures of a woman and on its contents pages notes which brands of cosmetics were used by the model is clearly giving those brands free advertising beyond what the space-user pays for. If the advertiser in this manner purchases what amounts to editorial mention, the publisher deceives the readers by letting the advertiser disguise his paid space. Furthermore, he is conditioning those who can thus be influenced to select one or more of those products when next they go shopping for cosmetics or whatever it may be. The influence may be indirect, almost subliminal, but it is there nevertheless. The buyer goes into a store, runs her eyes over shelves wondering which brand to buy, sees the now familiar name, reaches for the product and becomes a customer, perhaps for years. Or, if offended by the advertising, she may refuse to buy the product until she forgets her pique with its promotion.

Advertising of products and services in magazines represents another aspect of power and influence. Billions of dollars are spent by advertisers to reach potential customers among the readers of magazines and, as a corollary, publishers are constantly analyzing or testing the effectiveness of advertising in their particular magazines. Favorable results of such tests are, of course, put to good use by magazine promotion departments to attract potential advertisers—often by full-page ads in newspapers such as the New York *Times* and in advertising trade journals.

DIRECTIONS OF INFLUENCE

Two directions of magazine influence may be noted. The general or consumer book has a horizontal effect, since such a publication spreads widely (if not deeply) over the reading public. The specialized magazine's impact is vertical, because it is read by people in a comparatively narrow group, often stacked up in a single geographical area, as are the readers of certain industry, city, state or other regional periodicals.

Whether horizontal or vertical, the influence of magazines is noticeable through the letters-to-the-editor they receive. Although such letters are not scientific barometers because they can be stimulated by special-pleading groups or may even be the work of cranks, editors look to them as indicators of general reader reactions—indeed, experienced editors believe they can sense which letters are sincerely written. Those missives reporting on action taken as a result of reading the magazine are cherished and made much of by the promotion department. Such letters in turn influence editors and, if printed, their influence is further extended. Communications of this sort are read eagerly by many readers, so much so that most editors are loath to publish an issue without such copy and will even occasionally invite outsiders or subscribers to contribute for specific issues—nor is it unknown for the boss to ask the staff to write letters. In short, publishers' favorable attitudes toward letters should provide encouragement to readers to write more of them.

So distinct is the influence of magazines that such power is guarded. The more general the magazine the less it can afford to offend potent, particularized groups. Thus, for years criticism of Roman Catholics and Catholicism or Jews and Judaism have been avoided as too likely to alienate such important segments of readers and advertisers. Today sharp criticism of black citizens does not appear in consumer publications. But highly specialized magazines will venture to print it because they are read by persons sufficiently informed to tolerate incisive and well-intentioned discussion or evaluation of conditions within the field of their specialties.

A magazine of a certain church denomination, for instance, may carry critical views of that denomination. Dissenting or approving letters follow; a small civil war may seem to be brewing. However, usually the magazine goes on and eventually the differences are forgotten or reconciled. But let a multi-million circulation national magazine make similar assertions about that denomination's internal affairs. Harsh words will follow, antipathy toward the magazine develops, and subscriptions are cancelled. All this activity is the mark of influence, a degree of power to reach the minds of readers.

Through the letters they receive, the manuscripts submitted, conversations with readers among friends and visitors, and communications research on magazine influence (sparse as it may be), editors and publishers have been able to reach a few conclusions about magazine influence.

1. Readers change their minds slowly. They tend, in this country at least, to prefer to read over and over what they already know or believe. Despite the diversity of magazine content and viewpoint and the large number of periodicals available, readers develop loyalties to those that match their own viewpoints and will ignore those that publish opposing opinions. This tendency explains in part the huge circulations of conventional popular magazines and on the other hand the relatively minuscule distribution of periodicals that take vigorous but often unpopular positions. The exceptions are publications of moderate temper that coincide in social viewpoint with the bulk of the population and surround their views with appealing copy that cannot be abrasive, such as harmless human interest material, jokes, puzzles, bits of narrative, games and slice-of-life anecdotes.

2. Magazines exert influences of some sort, even though slight, merely by existing. Even an obscure little literary magazine affects some of its few hundred subscribers—those within its circle. Among the handful it reaches may be one literary genius, who through its encouragement may go on to become a force in literature. The biography of Ernest Hemingway

illustrates this point, as does that of many a poet who could not find hospitality in the commercial magazines. The history of *Poetry* magazine is full of examples.

3. Magazines exert influence over the short and long ranges, usually both. An election or a piece of legislation can be affected on the short term, a cultural trend can be launched and aided over the long. The muckrakers of past and present provide ample illustration. The classic instance from the beginning of the century is *McClure's,* which printed the work of three prime muckrakers: Ida M. Tarbell, Ray Stannard Baker and Lincoln Steffens. Their articles shook the nation with their revelations about corruption in the cities and monopolies in business. Upton Sinclair wrote a shelfload of books and scores of magazine articles along the same lines and became one of the world's most widely read authors.

The debate is not only over the power that magazines possess, but also over the nature and importance of their power—and whether that power is increasing or on the wane. For instance, is the power of magazines capable of bringing about social change in specific cases and affecting long-range trends in life styles in the cultural world or in business circles?

Is the power waning or growing? The answer depends upon where the power is being exerted as well as upon the precise time in our history. At the hour of writing this book the power of the general public appears to be largely at the personal level. The loss of major magazines in recent years has left an image of failure in the minds of some readers. The magazines, readers seem to be saying, are useful in their limited fashion but are no longer an important social force. They could not keep up with technological, social and economic developments. Added to these misconceptions is the prevalent critical attitude toward communications media in general that has existed since the mid-1960's, particularly in the handling of controversial issues.

Reporters have been imprisoned for refusal to reveal sources of information, press freedom has been placed under question by Supreme Court decisions, and broadcasting stations have been reminded that their licenses are issued by government and have been accused by government officials of unfair handling of news. The media in general have been attacked by elected officials and their advisers speaking at public gatherings, without provision of opportunity to reply. Departmental public relations offices in government agencies at times are uncooperative with press and other media people. On several occasions only those publications favorable to the administration in power have been invited to send their representatives for special briefings or social affairs. These practices, although most of them are old in American history and hardly restricted to any particular political party, have increased in the 1970's.

And the magazine industry, with some notable exceptions, seems indifferent to all this, perhaps because its publications have, on the whole, been thus treated somewhat more lightly than the other media. That may be because only a few are general news organs and they have given little offense, relatively, through articles and editorials—except for the minority of critical public affairs magazines and the periodicals of openly dissenting groups. To that portion of the public observing the stance and reaction to magazines, the power of magazines has diminished.

Yet there is another way of looking at the situation. So much concern today about what the media are saying may, in fact, be regarded as an indication of fear of communications' power. This interpretation may be gratifying to the media owners and their staffs but certain criticism of the press continues just the same, with magazines sharing a little in this attempt to deflate the communications media generally. It also may be said that it is not to the magazine industry's credit that it has not had to bear the brunt of the attacks on the press—in the light of previous episodes in American magazine history. There was a day when magazines engaged in libel suits were proud of themselves, for they were in some instances running risks for high purposes. Magazines silent in the face of social wrongdoing can make little claim to being courageous.

Therefore it may not be illogical to conclude that although as yet no in-depth studies have been conducted, the result may be that the pressures upon the other media have made the already cautious magazine publishers more cautious and the few outspoken ones more bold. The majority never have been the most courageous in the business, perhaps for obvious reasons of self-protection. The minority, having fought various restraints and even censorship for many years, has been emboldened by events to assert itself once more and more forcefully than ever—joined by a few of the more forceful well-heeled publications or those seeking a change in formula that might help to ward off further economic distress.

At this time, then, it may be concluded that magazines have power, although they are not extraordinarily powerful. What strength they may have in the future must be considered along with other aspects of magazine survival.

10

The Future

Magazines will continue to be printed for the time being, in the opinion of Dean Theodore Peterson of the School of Communications at the University of Illinois. However, in the early 1970's Dr. Peterson, author of a history of post-1900 U.S. periodicals, said he saw a possibility that magazines will be given away, delivered by newsboys and will be more tailored to the particular reader than they are today. The survivor will be the specialized periodical, he forecast. The big consumer book, in his view, is an anachronism.

Ample evidence supports Peterson. Hundreds of magazines are free to the reader now, their circulation classified as "controlled." For example *Folio,* begun in 1972 for the magazine industry itself, is sent without charge to more than 8,000 executives of magazine publishing firms and companies related to the industry. An expensively-produced publication, it depends almost entirely upon its advertising revenue to meet its costs.

Newsboy delivery is not new but never has been successful on a large scale in the past because of the expense as compared with postal charges. It is tried from time to time. At this writing, publishers of certain major magazines are using newsboys and also are testing delivery by the milkman through what is called the Magazine-Dairy Network Inc. These and other magazines—among them *Esquire, McCall's, Outdoor Life, Reader's Digest, Seventeen, Sports Afield, Good Housekeeping* and *Better Homes & Gardens*—also are experimenting with private mail delivery. If postal rates continue to climb, one or more of these methods may be the only way out, in the long run being less costly than depending upon the postal system.

Specialization, of course, has existed for years; it now is more intense than ever.

James Playsted Wood, another historian and for many years associated with Curtis, is also pessimistic about the large magazines. They now seem "vitiated and tardy," he wrote in 1971. The general magazine, he believes, no longer has the support of the public it once commanded, especially the general interest weekly, and he questions the need for it.

But Norman Cousins, in the first issue of his new magazine, *World*, in 1972 wrote:

> This first issue . . . is dedicated to the future of print . . . We are confident that print will not only endure but will continue to be a primary force in the life of the mind. Nothing yet invented meets the intellectual needs of the brain so fully as print. The ability of the mind to convert little markings on paper into meaning is one of the ways civilization receives its basic energy.

Long before that, however, Frank Luther Mott, the foremost historian of U.S. journalism, was pessimistic about a specific type of American magazine. Back in 1954 he wrote that "the next decade or two will see the obliteration of the distinction between the general literary monthly, and the low-priced book in its laminated cover. I think the general literary monthly is doomed; it is actually obsolescent at this time." Nearly 20 years later his prophecy had been fulfilled. Cousins believed Mott and changed the *Saturday Review of Literature* into a general interest magazine concerning arts and ideas. Such leading monthlies as the *Atlantic* and *Harper's* emphasize public affairs as much as they once did literature. *Commentary, Ramparts* and others have passed them as depicters of the current scene via non-fiction. In the meantime, a few magazine-book combinations (maga-books or bookazines) purview literature. So do scores of obscure little literary periodicals and substantial college-subsidized magazines, such as *Epoch* and *Massachusetts Review*. All are outlets for poets and story-

Cartoon by Edmund C. Arnold.

tellers. A few large periodicals make room for fiction, chiefly those aimed at women; a little of this fare no longer is of the namby-pamby type but concerned with such vital issues as race and war through settings and dialogue. Cinema, television and the paperback book killed off most of the larger, purely general literary magazines.

SOME PREDICTIONS

Most short-range forecasts speak about editorial content. A few mental leaps have been concerned with advertising, circulation, production and management. This author, in chapters for someone's else book issued in 1958, ventured predictions on those areas. The batting average on the short range was about 75 per cent.

Advertising was expected in the 1950's to grow in both volume and revenue. That indeed was the trend until the late 1960's and early 1970's, when for a large number of periodicals advertising volume decreased but revenue increased, because of rate rises. For some others both volume and revenue dropped. Now surcease appears to be coming, as in 1971 when tobacco advertising moved from television to the print media, adding to the latter's existing accounts or revenue. Since American publishing depends heavily upon the business world, directly or indirectly, a new short-range prediction rests upon the expectations of that world—in general those of economies in all departments, including advertising expenditures. Restraints on advertising will mean, for the time being, physically thinner periodicals and more failures. But a substantial number of magazines will continue because advertising is essential to business in general and magazines still offer access to specialized marketplaces too expensive to find and reach in any other way. Rates will continue to go up even though volume remains constant. Advertisers, on the other hand, will be offered more regional, demographic, split-run and other special editions or circulation breakdowns. (See App. 8, 9, 10, 11.)

Circulation, this writer thought in the 1950's, would increase. It did so with such success, under stimulus of costly promotion, rising educational levels, broadcasting and the inherent attractiveness of the magazine, that there came the time when some of the largest magazines cut their circulations voluntarily so as to reduce production costs. In the offing may be a more widely followed policy of limiting circulation so as not to let it get out of hand. That means modification of the traditional view that a big circulation is necessarily desirable and a mark of good journalistic health. It is, if a publisher can afford it—as several still can, for example *TV Guide* and *Playboy*. Special interest magazines, with intensely focused audiences, are unaffected by this change in emphasis on circulation because they are never aimed for mass distribution in the first place. (See App. 5.)

Production, the mechanical "manufacture" of the magazine and often the last area for change because of the printing industry's heavy investment in equipment, was thought in the late 1950's to be moving toward more special editions, small-size magazines, thinner issues, changes in frequency and printing experiments. The predictions were almost all accurate. Demographic and regional editions now are commonplace. As to size changes, some major periodicals have come down to 8 x 10 from 9 x 12. Offset rapidly became a prominent printing process, especially for small periodicals, but we now see what is called "dual printing," or more than one printing process used in a single issue. Magazines indeed became thinner, partly for lack of advertising and partly to reduce the ever-mounting production and mailing costs. Changes in frequency among major magazines failed to occur in large numbers. Instead, the few attempts led to disaster, as in the instance of *The Saturday Evening Post* (after its death it was revived as a quarterly in its more conventional format). Such efforts will continue, until dependable changes become generally acceptable.

The short-range prediction for management was that owners would emphasize specialized subject magazines rather than mass circulation periodicals. As we have seen in another chapter, that is precisely what has occurred since 1950 and continues at this writing, with almost weekly announcements of new magazines for old or new special areas. For instance, as this book was being written journalism acquired (*more*) magazine, parents of children with disabilities were given *The Exceptional Parent,* women of the black race were offered *Essence* and *Tuesday at Home.* Back-to-the-land enthusiasts were given two new magazines, *Plant Life* and *Yard and Fruit.* Circulation promotion was cut down as predicted, not only because it has become so costly but also because circulation itself became too expensive for certain consumer publications in particular. Mergers of magazines came about in almost wholesale fashion, also, as did exchanges of holdings between companies.

An unusual prediction that appeared in that 1958 book (*Journalism Tomorrow,* edited by Wesley C. Clark) was that "nothing significant will be accomplished to settle the ethical problem of the conflict between editorial and advertising content." For all practical purposes, little has. A few magazines in the years from 1958 to 1972 refused to take cigarette advertising, but others increased their acceptance as much as 300 per cent, after the tobacco companies had to leave television. Some advertisers attempted to capitalize on the new concern in the nation for man's environment. A few magazines were founded to deal with the problems of the ecology and a little space was given in large general magazines to these topics. But the bulk of dubious advertising themes continued, with the magazines selling space to the major polluters of the atmosphere while editorializing about the evils in the air and water about us. Complaints continued to come about the deceptive practices of the circulation and subscription companies working for magazine publishers.

An Electronics Future?

The more astute magazine managements, at the same time, have seen an electronic future. Time Inc., Condé Nast and Cowles (while still in the magazine business) have for years maintained broadcasting stations, to the point, in fact, where the federal government has charged monopolistic practices and divestment has taken place in some localities. These firms and others have interests in recording companies or in making cassettes and tapes. A few bind plastic records into their issues. Third-dimension photography has been used, but mainly in an occasional advertisement although it was regularly on the covers of the Cowles' now departed travel magazine, *Venture,* and once in a while it appeared in editorial matter in a trade or some other specialized periodical.

Professor James L. C. Ford of Southern Illinois University's School of Journalism, a former newsman and author of a book on specialized magazines, also has looked into the crystal ball. He concluded that "computer juke boxes" and ether waves may be used in the future, but he sees them producing "a page over which a man can reflect."

"When you roll out of bed, you'll turn the knob and get your Morning Magazine exactly as you ordered it the night before." Soon what he calls the Instant-Fac "will be running off your own special issue, expanding on the items for which you punched the buttons while watching." The tailored, individualized magazine will be ready for the subscriber to take with him as he goes toward his office or shop. During the day the news or other information will be up-dated. In the evening another edition comes forth. A gadget provides a simulcast or playback so there are visuals to go with the print-outs. Even swatches of textiles will be provided by the machine. The picture transmitted will be in third dimension and in color, with appropriate scents to match.

In their search for relief from rising production costs magazine entrepreneurs take such imaginative flights lightly. Instead they consider such possibilities as micropublishing. It appears to be a way out. But is it?

The content of a magazine can be published via microfilm more rapidly than on paper in some instances. The film can be distributed more cheaply, since it weighs far less and is much smaller; it also is easier to use in some ways, such as handling and storing.

Micropublishing can be one tenth the cost of regular printing of magazines on paper of 8½ x 11 size. Material requiring ten pounds of paper costs at least $3.00 to mail at parcel post rates. If it had been published on microfilm it would cost 24 cents first class.

Other advantages exist, but these are for the volume user rather than the ordinary reader, such as have auxiliary equipment available for making multiple copies of parts of a film.

Micropublishing is essentially a benefaction, therefore, for businesses, libraries and organizations which would be—and in many instances already are—equipped. But for the homeowner reader, it is unlikely that with even the simplest equipment he will find pictures of what he reads satisfactory. No one who has fumbled away minutes on mounting microfilms in elephantine reading machines, discovered torn film ends as he did so, or disliked the inability to mount and clip or use another machine to get impressions on paper will see such films as a general solution.

Still other forecasts are more optimistic. When the Batelle Memorial Institute conducted a $100,000 study of the graphic arts industry in 1968 it issued a forecast for 1990. As reported in *Printing Impressions,* it included a segment on the magazine printing business. It was cheering, declaring that "the periodical field will experience a continued and profitable existence." If the mass consumer magazines "change their approach and become—in effect—special interest magazines" was the qualifier, however. And by special interest the Batelle researchers meant magazines that "direct their editorial content to a single, particular subject matter or to a specific segment of the population . . ." They supported Professor Ford further by urging "The desirability of combining sensory (odor, feel, etc.) with visual output . . . Audio output should grow as a specialty item. These statements were applied particularly to business magazines.

PI reported that Batelle did not, however, "expect competitive communication systems" electronics to eliminate business publications (or even substantially reduce the usefulness of business publications. But it was forecasting for 1990. The year 2025 may be something else again.

A prediction for the long range: the magazine, as all readers until now have known it—that is, as an object made of paper and ink—will disappear except as a possession of historians, museum curators and sentimentalists who collected it from its paper days.

As a concept, however, the magazine will survive, but it will be expressed or represented in a different way than now. *Concept* means the formula of bringing together a wide variety of materials, of either general or special interest. The magazine concept is one of having either something for everyone or of providing many different kinds of content on a particular subject for those especially concerned about that topic.

The magazine of the distant future may come to readers, when reading can be accomplished through the non-use of printed words, by film, communicated via television tapes, or video cassettes, by some now unknown electronic device, or a combination of these. And these basic changes will affect its function.

To the Satisfied Reader such a forecast is disturbing. To most of the other readers it makes little difference. What readers want is the entertainment, the mental or emotional stimulation, the education or the information that magazines as a whole can provide. Whether the form changes is not important to them so long as the function is fulfilled with the least amount of trouble for them resulting from the new form. Witness, for example, the popularity of the magazine concept for television and radio ("The Magazine of the Air" or "60 Minutes").

Because the newspaper, the book and other printed matter also now appear to be on their way into history, in form if not function, the magazine is not alone in facing extinction as a physical object with the characteristics it now possesses. That fact may offer little satisfaction to readers habituated to the convenience of turning printed pages and communing with the ideas on those pages. But the evidence should be examined, distasteful as it may be.

MORE SPECULATION ON MEDIA OF THE FUTURE

Perhaps the most widely quoted forecaster of the end of print is Marshall McLuhan, the Canadian philosopher whose sometimes imprecise but provocative views jolted the communications world in 1961 when his book, *Understanding Media,* was published. Those views were discussed seriously and also were the sources of jokes (says one tribesman to another in a *New Yorker* cartoon: ". . . and when I finally did talk my tribe into learning to read, they read Marshall McLuhan!"). Some critics dismissed him as a sensationalist and popularizer, but his analyses and predictions continue to be studied by serious scholars of mass communications.

His central thesis was that the medium is the message—i.e., that the radio or television set, not only what it transmits, affects the listener or viewer the more, for it is an extension of man and possesses a formative power within itself. Just as the early machines changed society, so the media of communication in themselves also can change mankind.

McLuhan thereupon rated the various media as to whether they were hot or cool. The hot, he explained, are low in participation or completion by the audience and the cool are high. Speech, he noted, is cool because of low definition, i.e., since so little is given and so much has to be filled in by the listener. The print media, television and the telephone he ranked as cool, and radio and the motion picture as hot.

The conclusion to be drawn is that the cool print media are less effective extensions of ourselves than the hot media of radio and film (television appearing, in McLuhan's world, to be a combination of the two) and that print will in time give way to the others.

Considerable evidence has accumulated since McLuhan's heyday to support his thesis. Look at the trends of the 1970's. The great grand-children of today's under-30's, whether born in or out of marriage, will enter a world depending upon electronic devices for the communication of what heretofore has been printed on paper for direct transmission to the brain, including what now is not within the general public's easy financial reach, such as holography, facsimile telepaper and electronic video recordings.

Even today's children do not consider as novelties or experiments such communications tools as transistorized radio, use of satellites for transmission, motion pictures and television. Commonplace to them are cameras, teaching machines, records, audio cassettes, tapes, computers, telephones and copying machines. They do not need the printed word as did their great grandparents; the time is ahead when all except archivists will require it for every day existence.

Positive and negative reasons exist for the disappearance of printed journalism. Society cannot afford to go on with the expensive, clumsy and ecologically unsound process of producing billions of copies of magazines and other printed matter each year, most of which turn into waste paper. Seven million pounds of paper, 400,000 pounds of ink, 500 miles of wire and almost a week of continuous running of the presses go into the pro-duction of one issue of a magazine of four-million circulation, a Rochester Institute of Technology staff writer has noted. She pointed out, also, in *Reproduction Methods* magazine, that as many as 3,200 pages can be published on a 4 x 6″ transparency under the micropublishing system available through use of microforms (but as pointed out already, that system has its drawbacks also).

If—and it is an important if—an electronic device without such drawbacks can be devised, the home may be equipped so as to reproduce the life experience in sight and sound as now offered in print. Libraries already have become repositories not only of books, magazines, news-papers and other paperware but also of small boxes of micro materials, thereby saving enormous amounts of storage space and handling. Instead of reading history, future generations will witness and hear it from a screen, gaining their first impressions of the Duke of Marlborough, for example, from such a TV film as *The First Churchills,* or of United States history from Alistair Cooke's televised report, "America."

The business world, already deeply affected by technological change, will be forced by economic laws to make it possible for all society to live without print. And the public already is on the way to adjustment. Take, for example, those persons on all the continents who live more and more by sound. Several decades ago song writers saw what was happening and produced tunes with titles like "Music to Do Your Housework By." Factories and offices pipe in music to stimulate production. Taxi drivers and other motorists who dislike to think while driving, or fear they will fall asleep, have cassette or record players or radios or both in their cars. Busses, ships, planes and trains provide music, radio, television or movies for their passengers. Students are faced with advertisements for "Study Sounds" which allegedly improve grades. The student is told that the electronically-produced sound will "increase your concentration and improve your comprehension." It is possible for him, also, to study "at a faster rate," to quote the ads. He does it with an 8-track tape, cassette or long-play record. It is intended to help him keep his mind on his reading matter, which evidently no longer attracts him of its own accord. The spoken lesson may have been downgraded in the classroom, which becomes more and more a forum or discussion club and less and less a place for transmitting the acquired knowledge and experience of teachers. At the same time, however, the learning of a foreign language via electronics is booming. And television, film, slides and other non-printed media come more and more into use, for they are effective educational tools although only auxiliaries to the basic teaching methods.

Other practical evidence of the greater power of electronics than print comes from Dr. William H. Huggins, chairman of the Electrical Engineering Department of Johns Hopkins University. He sees the computer as a communication tool in that it can display visually complex systems and ideas. His views, as explained in 1971 in the *Johns Hopkins Journal,* are illustrated by an experiment made in 1964 at the Bell Laboratories. ". . . he converted to a computer-animated model the data compiled by a Harvard engineer who had devoted a lifetime of research to the workings of the inner ear," as the *Journal* reports it. Under Huggins' suggestions, the Bell engineers "created an astonishing pictorial representation of how the tiny components in the labyrinth of the inner ear respond to sound waves—a process that could be visualized in no other way."

Thus the computer increasingly is becoming a serious and important factor in human communication, creating more and more independence of the printed word. It emphasizes the symbolic rather than just the visual, as does television, but is capable of both. So Huggins says that "the function of TV and the computer might be integrated into some new device so as to be most useful and helpful in man's intellectual development." The *Journal's* unnamed writer said that Huggins "envisions a device which would be like television in that it could generate the images of a great variety. It would also be like a computer in that it would invite active participation of the viewer by enabling him to enter into the generation and control of the material being displayed." Such a system, it is pointed out, "would for the first time give man the ability to produce images with the same facility that he has always been able to produce speech."

Thus the magazine gradually gives way. Just when it will be superseded depends upon the speed with which the engineers can produce cheaply enough the equipment needed. These include the attachments to home sets that will hold television programs for later viewing, now available but too costly for average users; the projectors to throw on the wall-screens pictures that have been transmitted by radio, and the pocket devices that will receive direct voice communication from reasonable distances, and all the other hard- and soft-ware involved in these electronic miracles of communications. It will depend, also, upon the speed with which the new generations are weaned away from print by the domination of electronics.

A
Supplementary Reading List

Selective and Annotated

SINCE THE 1950's the literature about magazines in the United States has been enriched greatly, although it still is far from adequate in many areas of magazine publication. Readers as well as managers, nevertheless, now may examine the industry more deeply than ever before.

The enrichment in certain categories was brought about by more intensive studies of magazine publishing in the universities and colleges, the growth of the industry and the public interest in movements within the business, such as the demise of several old and widely-known magazines, the rise to affluence of various newcomers in the field, and publishing figures whose lives have made readable copy.

Included here is a representative selection of, for the most part, the more recent books pertinent to an evaluation of magazinedom and magazinists. Older books omitted from the list may be traced through several reference works, including:

The Literature of Journalism, by Warren C. Price (Minneapolis: University of Minnesota Press, 1959)

An Annotated Journalism Bibliography, by Warren D. Price and Calder M. Pickett (Minneapolis: University of Minnesota Press, 1970)

Basic Books in the Mass Media, by Eleanor Blum (Urbana: University of Illinois Press, 1972)

The Journalist's Bookshelf, by Roland E. Wolseley (New York: Chilton, 1961, Seventh Edition)

Useful supplements to these books that provide new titles regularly are: *Journalism Quarterly, Columbia Journalism Review, Quill & Scroll, The Quill* and *School Press Review.*

BIOGRAPHY AND MEMOIRS

Bliven, Bruce. *Five Million Words Later: An Autobiography.* New York: Day, 1970.
 Although best known for his 30 years as editor of *The New Republic,* the author also was editor of the New York *Globe* and U.S. correspondent for the *Guardian* of Manchester, England; a realistic and sensitive account, with evaluation of the media.
Chase, Edna Woolman and Ilka Chase. *Always in Vogue.* New York: Doubleday, 1954.
 Always intimate in tone, this autobiography of the long-time editor of *Vogue* (written with Mrs. Chase's actress-author daughter) goes behind the scenes of the Conde' Nast firm to show its operations and its better known editors and writers before mid-century.
Fonzi, Gaeton. *Annenberg: A Biography of Power.* New York: Weybright & Talley, 1970.
 Walter H. Annenberg, publisher of *Seventeen* and *TV Guide* and until recently of several large newspapers as well as the American ambassador to Great Britain, is portrayed here by a biographer critical of his policies and methods.
Gingrich, Arnold. *Nothing But People.* New York: Crown, 1971.
 The recollections of the first editor of *Coronet* and *Esquire* and still publisher of the latter; filled with anecdotes and first-hand reports on the rise and development of his own and other magazines and comments on various writers and editors.
Gould, Bruce and Beatrice Blackmar Gould. *American Story.* New York: Harper & Row, 1968.
 Former joint editors of *The Ladies' Home Journal* and husband and wife, the authors report on their careers with the original Curtis Publishing Company, whose management policies in their time comes off with sharp criticism, as does Madison Avenue.
Humes, Joy D. *Oswald Garrison Villard: Liberal of the 1920's.* Syracuse, N.Y.: Syracuse University Press, 1960.
 In a study of the liberal political movement of the post World War I period, the author focuses on Villard, long the editor of *The Nation* and a prolific writer on the press; other sources are Villard's autobiography, *Fighting Years* (New York: Harcourt, Brace, 1939) and Michael Wreszin's *Oswald Garrison Villard: Pacifist at War.* (Bloomington, Ind.: Indiana University Press, 1965).
Kobler, John. *Luce: His Time, Life and Fortune.* New York: Doubleday, 1968.
 A former *Time* staff member presents a balanced view of Henry Robinson Luce; useful also for a report on the policies of *Time* and of Time Inc.; see also *The Ideas of Henry Luce,* edited by John K. Jessup (New York: Atheneum, 1969) and *Luce and His Empire* by W. A. Swanberg (New York: Scribner's, 1972).

Kramer, Dale. *Ross and the New Yorker.* New York: Doubleday, 1951.
Both Harold Ross and his magazine were so extraordinary that almost any book on them would be good reading; despite lack of cooperation from his subject in gathering material, Kramer reveals the man and also accounts for such staff luminaries as Robert Benchley and James Thurber.

Leckie, Janet. *A Talent for Living: The Story of Henry Sell, An American Original.* New York: Hawthorn, 1970.
Henry Blackman Sell, editor successively of *The Delineator, Harper's Bazaar* and *Town & Country,* was 80 in 1959 and still hale when this book was published; an admiring and handsomely illustrated account, it is of deep interest to magazinists as well as to readers among the beautiful people.

Lent, John A. *Newhouse, Newspapers, Nuisances.* New York: Exposition, 1966.
A semi-biography of the owner of *Vogue, Glamour, Mademoiselle* and other magazines as well as numerous other media of communication; critical of the Newhouse labor and financial policies in particular.

Lyon, Peter. *Success Story: The Life and Times of S.S. McClure.* New York: Scribner's, 1963.
One of the most thorough yet readable biographies of a magazine leader, this volume is a study of the founder of the influential *McClure's* and of early Sunday magazine supplements; the full story of the muckrakers is here.

Rudwick, Elliott M. *W. E. B. Du Bois: Propagandist of the Negro People.* New York: Atheneum, 1968.
Du Bois established five magazines, including *The Crisis* and *Phylon,* still going; his extraordinary career as sociologist, scholar, journalist, public speaker, and political leader comes through; see also Mrs. Du Bois' memoirs, *His Day is Marching On* (Philadelphia: Lippincott, 1971) and his *Autobiography* (New York: International, 1968).

Snow, Carmel with Mary Louise Aswell. *The World of Carmel Snow.* New York: McGraw-Hill, 1962.
The reminiscences of the haughty journalistic fashion queen who ruled *Harper's Bazaar;* often gossipy and sentimental but never tedious; some sidelights on *Vogue* also.

GROUPS OF MAGAZINISTS

Davenport, Walter and James C. Derieux. *Ladies, Gentlemen and Editors.* Garden City, N.Y.: Doubleday, 1960.
A lively recounting of several dozen more or less familiar biographies, including Sarah Josepha Hale, of *Godey's,* Edward Bok of *The Ladies' Home Journal,* Frank Leslie of the *Illustrated Weekly,* and Cyrus H. K. Curtis, founder of the Curtis group.

HISTORY

Emery, Edwin. *The Press and America*. Englewood Cliffs, N.J.: Prentice-Hall, 1972. Third Edition.

Because the latest available general history of magazines stops at 1968, this "interpretative history of the mass media" is valuable since it is up to date and also in that it places magazines in perspective with the nation's history and that of the media with which they co-exist; its third edition makes it the outstanding communications work of its kind; see also Frank Luther Mott's *American Journalism* (New York: Macmillan, 1962, Third Edition).

Mott, Frank Luther. *A History of American Magazines*. Cambridge, Mass.: Belknap Press of Harvard University Press. Five Volumes.

The outstanding scholarly work on U.S. magazines, winning its author the Pulitzer, Bancroft and other prizes; it is an amazingly thorough, meticulously accurate and readable account; the volumes were published in 1930, 1938, 1957, and 1968; the latter, edited by Dean Mott's daughter, includes a 250-page index to all five.

Peterson, Theodore. *Magazines in the Twentieth Century*. Urbana: University of Illinois Press, 1964. Second Edition.

Picking up more or less where Mott left off, Peterson accounts for the developments up to the early 1960's; the decade since leaves this sound book in need of revision.

Tebbel, John. *The American Magazine: A Compact History*. New York: Hawthorn, 1969.

Logically organized, it is intended for readers rather than scholars and gives the highlights in most readable fashion.

INDIVIDUAL MAGAZINES OR COMPANIES

Bainbridge, John. *Little Wonder*. New York: Reynal & Hitchcock, 1946.

The "little wonder" is *Reader's Digest,* which Bainbridge found to be a baneful influence on American life up the mid-1940's; for a more kindly but evidently authorized report see James Playsted Wood's *Of Lasting Interest* (New York: Doubleday, 1967. Second Edition).

Cousins, Norman. *Present Tense*. New York: McGraw-Hill, 1967.

Not a history, yet a 60-page opening chapter provides as much as is so far available outside a doctoral dissertation by Sherilyn Cox Bennion on *Saturday Review;* the remainder is a collection of editorials by Cousins and others; he was editor when the volume was published; all reveal the wide scope and liberal views.

Elson, Robert T. *Time Inc.: The Intimate History of a Publishing Enterprise, 1923–1941*. New York: Atheneum, 1968. Volume I.

Although the authorized history of this large firm, it faces some of the common criticisms of newsmagazines and of *Time* in particular; letters and biographies of individuals are included.

Goldberg, Joe. *Big Bunny: The Inside Story of Playboy*. New York: Ballantine, 1967.

An entertaining account of the men's magazine and its founder, Hugh M. Hefner; the author writes with considerable reverence for the financial success that has favored most Hefner enterprises; see also William S. Banowsky's *It's a Playboy World* (Old Tappan, N.J.: Revell, 1969).

Gussow, Don. *Divorce Corporate Style*. New York: Ballantine, 1972.

Behind the scenes at Cowles Communications, particularly the sale to that firm of the author's trade magazine company and its repurchase by him before the magazine difficulties at Cowles; here also is background on the *Look* disaster; the vignettes of Mike Cowles and other management figures are revealing.

Wood, James Playsted. *The Curtis Magazines*. New York: Ronald Press, 1971.

A condensed history of *The Saturday Evening Post* and other Curtis periodicals as well as of the company and its administrators; the author himself was at Curtis from 1946 to 1962; it goes through the *Post's* death under the old firm. See also Joseph C. Goulden's *The Curtis Caper* (New York: Putnam, 1965) for an early analysis; Matthew J. Culligan's *The Curtis-Culligan Story* (New York: Crown, 1970) for the viewpoint of a president striving to save the firm; Martin S. Ackerman's *The Curtis Affair* (Los Angeles: Nash, 1970), in which the last president gives his side; and Otto Friedrich's *Decline and Fall* (New York: Harper & Row, 1970), the most thorough and readable report of the complicated story.

EVALUATION

Ruckner, Bryce W. *The First Freedom*. Carbondale, Ill.: Southern Illinois University Press, 1968.

Although it considers the mass media in general, it includes the freedoms enjoyed or neglected by magazines; the author fears monopolistic tendencies and looks to weekly newspapers and large foundations as the way out.

Schacht, John H. *The Journals of Opinion and Reportage*. New York: Magazine Publishers Association, 1966.

An assessment of *The Nation, National Review* and other such periodicals; the views of certain leaders are traced.

Shulman, Irving. *"Jackie!" The Exploitation of a First Lady*. New York: Trident, 1970.

Actually an exposé of the fan magazines, using the treatment of Mrs. Jacqueline Onassis as a case in point; the readers are depicted and the editorial motives clearly shown.

Woodward, Helen. *The Lady Persuaders*. New York: Obolensky, 1960.

From a background of service with three of the largest women's magazines, and as an agency account executive, the author takes mighty swats at the weaknesses she saw in them during her time; she dislikes the "pretense . . . of lofty . . . noble enterprise" when she knows "it is simply a business."

MAGAZINES IN GENERAL

Wolseley, Roland E. *Understanding Magazines*. Ames, Iowa: Iowa State University Press, 1969. Second Edition.
> The specialized magazine is singled out as the survivor into the near future in this general survey covering history, various departmental operations, major types of periodicals, and vocational interests.

Wood, James Playsted. *Magazines in the United States*. New York: Ronald, 1971. Third Edition.
> A description, emphasizing history of magazines and the background from which they sprang, examination of various types and their place in the social scene; the author is pessimistic about the general magazine's future. See also James L. C. Ford's *Magazines for Millions* (Carbondale, Ill.: Southern Illinois University Press, 1969) for a survey of specialized magazines.

MISCELLANEOUS

Clark, Wesley C., ed. *Journalism Tomorrow*. Syracuse, N.Y.: Syracuse University Press, 1958.
> Forecasts about magazines and other media prepared in 1957 by university teachers stand up well in the short run predictions; later prophecies are still to be tested.

Current Editorial Problems: A Seminar. New York: Magazine Publishers Association, 1969.
> The text of what was said by outstanding editors at six consecutive sessions of the seminar, sponsored by the American Society of Magazine Editors on such problems as the change in women readers, the editor's posture toward social revolution, and starting a new magazine; the speakers included Osborn Elliott, William F. Buckley, Jr., Gerry Rhoads, Betsy Blackwell, Clay Felker, Richard E. Deems, Herbert Mayes, and other VIP's.

Dennis, Everette E., ed. *The Magic Writing Machine*. Eugene: University of Oregon, 1971.
> Ten articles about the new journalism: its origin and practitioners. See also *The New Journalism* by Michael L. Johnson (Lawrence: University Press of Kansas, 1971).

Garberson, John W. *"A Limited Number of Advertising Pages"*. Lexington, Ky.: Journalism Monographs, Association for Education in Journalism, 1972. No. 25.
> A report on the background of the decision by the *Reader's Digest* to open its pages to advertising; the author, now a journalism teacher, was on the magazine's staff at the time and gives behind-the-scenes data.

Schuneman, R. Smith, ed. *Photographic Communication: Principles, Problems and Challenges of Photojournalism*. New York: Hastings House, 1972.
> A unique anthology selected from 15 years of the Wilson Hicks International Conference on Photocommunication Arts, including several chapters from Wilson Hicks' *Words and Pictures*, now out of print.

Appendices

1

COMPARATIVE GENERAL STATISTICS FOR PERIODICAL INDUSTRY 1968–1971

	All employees		Production workers			Value added by manufacture	Cost of materials	Value of shipments	Capital expenditures, new	End-of-year inventories
	Number	Payroll	Number	Man-hours	Wages					
	(1,000)	(million dollars)	(1,000)	(millions)	(million dollars)	(million dollars)	(million dollars)	(million dollars)	(million dollars)	(million dollars)
1968	83.5	692.7	16.9	29.8	94.9	2,048.2	1,306.7	3,341.9	62.1	207.7
1969	85.1	727.7	16.0	29.1	105.6	2,118.0	1,360.3	3,468.4	73.6	222.0
1970	76.9	691.3	13.7	27.6	102.2	1,930.6	1,210.6	3,157.9	(67.7) *	198.8
1971	71.4	684.9	13.7	25.1	101.5	2,013.4	1,241.3	3,242.0	107.0	201.2

* A limited reliability estimate.

Source: *Annual Survey of Manufactures,* 1968, 1969, 1970, 1971, U.S. Department of Commerce.

2

VALUE OF SHIPMENTS—PERIODICALS 1967–1970
Receipts from subscriptions and sales and from advertising

		1967	1968	1969	1970
			(million dollars)		
General periodicals	A.	593.5	652.2	685.4	722.2
	B.	879.5	887.1	909.9	859.6
Specialized business and periodicals professional	A.	149.6	186.9	216.2	195.1
	B.	524.9	544.5	574.9	522.0
Farm periodicals	A.	11.3	14.7	16.6	22.8
	B.	45.7	55.0	58.7	43.6
Other periodicals	A. + B.	284.2	299.1	246.9	267.0
Periodicals not specified by kind	A. + B.	179.5	162.5	188.0	165.5
All periodicals		2,668.2	2,802.0	2,896.6	2,797.8

Code: A. Subscriptions and sales revenue
B. Advertising revenue

Source: Annual Survey of Manufactures, 1967, 1968, 1969, 1970, U.S. Department of Commerce.

3

MAGAZINE VITAL STATISTICS 1962–1971 *

Year	Sold, Merged or Discontinued	New
1962	10	41
1963	17	50
1964	6	41
1965	17	73
1966	18	70
1967	9	115
1968	22	101
1969	17	100
1970	24	86
1971	20	76
10-year total	160	753

* Note: These figures are not inclusive because vital statistics on specialized periodicals or non-commercial magazines are not always reported to MPA.

Source: Magazine Publishers Association records, 1972.

4

CLASSIFICATION GROUPINGS OF CONSUMER MAGAZINES

Classification	Example
Airline Inflight	*The American Way*
Almanacs & Directories	*The Old Farmer's Almanac*
Arts and Antiques	*Art in America*
Automotive	*Motor Trend*
Aviation	*Flying*
Babies	*Your New Baby*
Boating and Yachting	*Yachting*
Brides	*Modern Bride*
Business and Finance	*Business Week*
Campers, Recreational Vehicles, Mobile Homes and Trailers	*Mobile Living*
Camping and Outdoor Recreation	*Northeast Outdoors*
Children's	*Jack and Jill*
Civic (Male)	*Kiwanis*
College and Alumni	*American Alumni Magazine*
Comics and Comic Technique	Gold Key Comics Group
Crafts, Hobbies and Models	*World Coins*
Dancing	*Square Dancing*
Detective	*Master Detective*
Dogs and Pets	*Dog World*
Dressmaking and Needlework	*Singer Showcase*
Editorial and Classified Advertising	Classified, Inc.
Education and Teacher	*Early Years*
Entertainment Guides and Programs	*Cue*
Epicurean	*Bon Appetit*
Fashions	*Vogue*
Finance	*Stock Market*
Fishing and Hunting	*Field & Stream*
Fraternal, Professional Groups Service Clubs and Associations	*Hadassah*
Gardening (Home)	*Home Garden*
General Editorial (Class Oriented)	*Natural History*
General Editorial (Mass Oriented)	*Reader's Digest*
General Editorial (Paperback)	Fawcett Ad Inserts
Health	*Life & Health*
Home Service and Home	*American Home*
Horses and Breeding	*Western Horseman*
Labor—Trade Union	*Labor Press*

Classification (cont.)	Example (cont.)
Literary—Book Reviews, and Writing Technique	*The Writer*
Mechanics and Science	*Popular Mechanics*
Men's	*Saga*
Metropolitan	*The Washingtonian*
Military and Naval	*The Retired Officer*
Movie, Radio, TV and Records Personalities	*T.V. Star Parade*
Music	*Opera News*
Mystery, Adventure and Science Fiction	*Fate*
Nature and Ecology	*Audubon*
News	*Jet*
Newspaper Comic Supplements	*Puck*
Newspaper Distributed Magazines	*Parade*
Photography	*Camera 35*
Physical Sciences	*Sky & Telescope*
Political and Social Topics	*Africa Report*
Professional	*Clubwoman*
Religious and Denominational	*Sign*
Romance	*True Romance*
Senior Citizens	*Harvest Years*
Society	*Town & Country*
Sports	*World Tennis*
Travel	*Travel & Leisure*
TV and Radio	*Radio Electronics*
Veterans	*VFW*
Women's	*Lady's Circle*
Women's Fashions, Beauty and Grooming	*Glamour*
Youth	*American Girl*

Source: *Standard Rate & Data Service Consumer Magazine and Farm Publication Rates & Data.* Vol. 54, No. 11, Nov. 23, 1972.

5

GROWTH OF ABC CONSUMER MAGAZINES 1955–1971

Year	Number of Magazines or Groups	One-Issue Circulation
1955	260	166,286,858
1957	281	180,965,428
1959	269	182,310,061
1961	270	192,225,088
1963	275	202,771,860
1965	279	211,659,541
1967	283	229,142,899
1969	298	237,024,860
1971	305	243,124,372

ABC: Audit Bureau of Circulations
MPA: Magazine Publishers Association

Source: ABC reports on general and farm magazines (excluding comics) for first six months of each year, as compiled by MPA in 1972.

6

BUSINESS MAGAZINE PUBLISHING FIRMS WITH TEN OR MORE PERIODICALS *

Firm	Number of Periodicals
McGraw-Hill, Inc.	27
Harcourt Brace Jovanovich, Inc.	24 **
Cahners Publishing Co., Inc.	23
Chilton Co.	21
Dun-Donnelley Publishing Corp.	13 ***
Industrial Publishing Co.	12

* Covers only members of American Business Press, Inc.
** Includes Harvest Publishing Co. periodicals
*** Includes an Industrial Research Inc. periodical

7

PERCENTAGE OF INCREASE IN READERSHIP OF EDITORIAL MATTER—1959–1969

MEN		WOMEN	
Noted	+8%	General Magazines	
Read some	+11%	Noted	+9%
Read most	+7%	Read some	+9%
		Read most	+8%
		Women's Magazines (1960–1969)	
		All editorial	+15%
		All advertising	+23%

Source: Daniel Starch & Staff, Inc., as cited by Magazine Publishers Association, 1972, in *Rediscovering Magazines.*

8

TEN LEADING MAGAZINE ADVERTISERS—1971

Rank	Advertiser	Total Magazine Expenditure
1	General Motors Corp.	$29,207,787
2	Philip Morris, Inc.	27,336,936
3	R.J. Reynolds Industries, Inc.	24,805,519
4	British-American Tobacco Co., Ltd.	24,575,324
5	Ford Motor Co.	22,778,023
6	Distillers Corp.—Seagrams, Ltd.	22,054,157
7	Sears, Roebuck & Co.	22,052,685
8	Bristol-Myers Co.	18,746,927
9	Liggett & Myers, Inc.	17,139,940
10	General Foods Corp.	15,168,501

Source: *Rediscovering Magazines* (Magazine Publishers Association, 1972, p. 27).

9

NUMBER OF ADVERTISERS SPENDING $25,000 OR MORE IN MAGAZINES—1950–1971

Year	Number
1950	1,793
1955	2,148
1960	2,262
1965	2,337
1970	2,297
1971	2,330

Source: Publishers Information Bureau

10

GROWTH OF REGIONAL ADVERTISING IN MAGAZINES—1959–1971

Year	Advertising Revenue	% of Total Revenue
1959	$ 42,629,531	5.4%
1962	114,381,512	13.1
1965	163,760,729	15.1
1968	199,963,964	16.7
1971	222,722,985	17.8

Source: Publishers Information Bureau

11

STABILITY OF MAGAZINE ADVERTISING COSTS—1966–1971

Year	Cost per thousand index *	
	Black and White Page	Four-Color Page
1966	100	100
1967	99	99
1968	99	99
1969	103	103
1970	105	104
1971	106	105

* Cost per page per thousand circulation in 1966 equals 100.

Source: MPA Cost Series—50 Leading Magazines, as reproduced in *Rediscovering Magazines,* 1972.

12

U.S. PERIODICALS WITH ONE MILLION OR MORE CIRCULATION

Amalgamated Pictorial
  Supplement *
American Home
American Legion
Argosy
Awake
Baby Talk
Better Homes and
  Gardens
Boys' Life
Changing Times
Consumer Reports
Cosmopolitan
Decision
Ebony
Elks
Esquire
Family Circle
Family Weekly *
Farm Journal
Field & Stream
Glamour
Good Housekeeping
Holiday

House and Garden
Junior Scholastic
Ladies' Home Journal
McCall's
Mad
Mechanix Illustrated
Motion Picture
National Geographic
New York *Times Book*
  Review *
New York *Times*
  Magazine *
Newstime
Newsweek
Outdoor Life
Parade *
Parents'
Penthouse
Photoplay
Playboy
Popular Mechanics
Popular Science
  Monthly
Progressive Farmer

Reader's Digest
Redbook
Scouting
Seventeen
Sport
Sports Afield
Sports Illustrated
Successful Farming
Time
Today's Education
Travel & Leisure
True
Tuesday *
Tuesday at Home *
TV Guide
TV Radio Mirror
Upper Room
U.S. News and World
  Report
V.F.W. Magazine
Watchtower
Woman's Day
Workbasket

* Magazine supplement of newspapers

Source: Ayer *Directory*, 1972; *Standard Rate & Data Service*, 1972 issues; publisher's reports.

13

TEN HIGHEST CIRCULATING INDIVIDUAL
CONSUMER PERIODICALS *

Name	Circulation
Reader's Digest	17,827,661 **
TV Guide	16,410,858
Woman's Day	8,191,731
Better Homes & Gardens	7,996,050
Family Circle	7,889,587
McCall's	7,516,960
National Geographic	7,260,179
Ladies' Home Journal	7,014,251
Playboy	6,400,573
Good Housekeeping	5,801,446

* Excluding group and newspaper supplement circulations.
** U.S. circulation only.

Source: *SRDS Consumer Magazine and Farm Publication Rates & Data,* Nov. 23, 1972. Vol. 54, no. 1.

Index

DAVID GLENN HUNT
MEMORIAL LIBRARY
GALVESTON COLLEGE

DAVID GLENN HUNT
MEMORIAL LIBRARY
GALVESTON COLLEGE